T0151999

Making it in the Political Blogosphere

Making it in the
Political Blogosphere

The World's Top Political Bloggers
Share the Secrets to Success

TANNI HAAS

The Lutterworth Press

The Lutterworth Press
P.O. Box 60
Cambridge
CB1 2NT
United Kingdom

www.lutterworth.com
publishing@lutterworth.com

ISBN: 978 0 7188 9277 7

British Library Cataloguing in Publication Data
A record is available from the British Library

Contents

Acknowledgements

This book wouldn't exist were it not for the generosity of spirit of the 20 political bloggers profiled here. They willingly took time from their busy schedules to speak with me about their craft. Thank you. I'd also like to thank Adrian Brink of The Lutterworth Press for believing in me and my project. Finally, I want to thank the two people closest to my heart, my beautiful wife, Nicole, and son, Milan. You make it all worthwhile.

Introduction:
The Rise and Influence of the Political Blogging A-list

While the technology behind blogs has been around since the early 1990s, blogging became increasingly popular in the late 1990s with the introduction of freely available and user-friendly software like *Blogger*, *LiveJournal*, and *Weblogger*.[1] Since then, the number of blogs has grown exponentially. According to one study, two new blogs are created every second.[2] While estimates of the overall number of blogs differ widely, research indicates that the fastest-growing category — political blogs[3] — currently stands at around 1.3 million.[4]

The 1.3 million political bloggers, of whom the vast majority are ordinary people with a passion for politics, use their blogs to report original news from events they've personally witnessed, analyze and comment on the reporting by mainstream news media, and champion their own political causes. Political bloggers often encourage their readers to support particular political candidates and parties, by featuring political ads, soliciting campaign contributions, circulating online petitions, and posting information about upcoming rallies and votes.[5] Simply put, political bloggers use their blogs to express their political beliefs, interact with like-minded individuals, inform their readers, and influence the political world around them.[6]

The incredible growth in political blog writing is mirrored in the number of people who read them. While an impressive 44% of all Americans have read political blogs,[7] tens of millions do so daily. Studies show that political blog readers spend more time reading blogs than do readers of any other kind of blog (five blogs a day, up to 10 hours a week)[8] with many political blog enthusiasts spending several hours daily in the blogosphere.[9]

The influence of political blogs reaches far beyond their immediate readership. Political blog readers tend to be politically active individuals who engage others in online and interactive conversations about what they've read, thereby serving as opinion-leaders for countless other people.[10]

Even more significant than the sheer number of people who read and are influenced by political blogs is the importance people attach to them. Studies have found that political blog readers consider such blogs more trustworthy sources of information than they do any other mainstream news media, including online and offline newspapers, television, and radio. Political blogs are considered more trustworthy because they provide access to a broader spectrum of issues than is available in the mainstream news media; cover those issues in greater depth, with more independence and points of view; and present them in a manner that's more understandable and relevant to readers.[11]

The Stature and Influence of the Political Blogging A-List

While more than a million people have political blogs, a select few wield enormous influence within the political blogosphere and in politics. Variously referred to as the "political blogging A-list,"[12] the "influentials,"[13] or even the "kings and queens of blogland,"[14] these bloggers attract the majority of political blog readers, set the agenda for the many smaller blogs, are widely read by mainstream journalists and, as I describe in the next section, exert a strong impact on politics.

Political blog readership isn't evenly distributed as the top blogs attract most of the readers. One study revealed that the top 10 blogs account for 48% of readers.[15] The 20 bloggers featured in this book, all of whom belong to the political blogging A-list, have a combined daily audience of 2–3 million readers.

The top blogs aren't only read by a large and ever growing audience; they also influence what the rest of the political blogosphere blogs about. This becomes clear when one considers how political bloggers link to one another. If there were no agenda-setters in the political blogosphere, all political blogs would have roughly the same number of incoming links from other blogs. Yet, research shows, a few top blogs receive the bulk of incoming links. A study of more than 400 political blogs found that, while the top 12 blogs attracted 20% of all incoming blog links, the top 50 blogs attracted 50% of all such links.[16]

The influence of the top blogs goes beyond the mass of smaller blogs. Mainstream journalists — political reporters and columnists in particular — regularly read political blogs, often several blogs daily. They do so to gather ideas for future stories, hear what's being said in the political blogosphere about their reporting, and to gauge public reactions to major news events.[17]

But journalists don't just read any political blog they happen to encounter. Like political blog readers, their reading is also focused on a few top blogs. A study of 140 journalists employed by national and local news organizations in the U.S. found that the ten most widely read blogs accounted for 54% of those mentioned. Among journalists working for national news organizations, this bias was even more pronounced: the ten most widely read blogs accounted for almost 75% of those mentioned.[18]

Journalists' blog reading behavior is quite logical. Since the top blogs attract the majority of political blog readers, and set the agenda for countless smaller blogs, journalists only need to read these blogs to get a relatively accurate impression of public (and blogger) opinion with respect to certain issues.

The Political Blogging A-list's Impact on Politics

Most impressively, there are many examples of how top political bloggers have had an impact on politics, either indirectly through their influence on mainstream journalists or directly through their blogging.

The first and most widely cited incident of political blogger influence has become known as the Trent Lott affair (or Lottgate.)[19] On December 5, 2002, a large number of political dignitaries were gathered in the Dirksen Senate Office Building to celebrate Senator Strom Thurmond's (R-SC) one-hundred birthday. Many of Thurmond's Republican colleagues spoke, praising the Senate's longest-serving member for his many accomplishments over a long career. But one of Thurmond's colleagues, Senate Majority Leader Trent Lott (R-MS), went one step further. During his remarks, Lott said that his home state of Mississippi was proud to have voted for Thurmond when, in 1948, he'd run for president as a third-party candidate on a segregationist platform: "I want to say this about my state: When Strom Thurmond ran for president, we voted for him. We're proud of it. And if the rest of the country had followed our lead, we wouldn't have had all these problems over all these years."

Although Lott's controversial remarks were broadcast live on *C-SPAN*, they elicited no reactions among the many mainstream journalists who covered the event. In fact, none of the major television networks mentioned his remarks on the prime-time news shows that evening, nor did the major newspapers the next day.

It was only after Lott's remarks were heavily criticized by several top conservative and liberal bloggers, who also called for his resignation, that the mainstream news media began to take notice. On December 10, or fully five days after the event, the *New York Times* covered the story for the first time, and each of the nightly network news shows discussed Lott's remarks.

As the story continued to grow, and more political bloggers and mainstream journalists started to cover it, insisting that Lott be held accountable for his remarks, both the White House and other Republican senators began to distance themselves from Lott who, under considerable party pressure, resigned his position as Senate Majority Leader on December 20. The political blogging A-list's ability to force the story into the mainstream news, which ultimately forced Lott to relinquish his leadership position, led one noted observer to call the Trent Lott affair "the Internet's first scalp."[20]

The Trent Lott affair is only one of many examples of the power of the political blogging A-list to effect political change through its influence on the mainstream news media. Even more impressively, it also has the power to do so directly through its blogging.

In 2005, President Bush nominated White House Counsel Harriet Miers to replace retiring Supreme Court Justice Sandra Day O'Connor. However, shortly after the Oval Office ceremony, top conservative bloggers began to challenge her suitability as a Supreme Court Justice, questioning her allegiance to core conservative principles. The attacks were so strong that Bush, a little more than three weeks later, withdrew her nomination. When Bush subsequently nominated Appeals Court Justice Samuel Alito instead, the Republican National Committee held a series of meetings with top conservative bloggers to ensure that this time, they would stand united behind the White House's chosen nominee. The meetings featured various White House officials, including Deputy Chief of Staff and trusted Bush advisor Karl Rove, as well as several prominent senators.[21]

Two years later, in 2007, the top liberal blog *Talking Points Memo* broke the story of how the Department of Justice, under the leadership of Attorney General Alberto Gonzales, had fired eight US district attorneys for what appeared to be politically motivated reasons. *Talking Point Memo*'s extensive coverage of the story caught the attention of the House Judiciary Committee which decided to hold hearings, ultimately leading to Gonzales' resignation.[22]

More recently, during the 2008 presidential election, another top liberal blog, *The Huffington Post*, posted a video from a San Francisco fundraiser in which then-senator Barack Obama said that Pennsylvania voters, who would be voting in the upcoming primaries, were "bitter" people who "cling to guns or religion." The public response to Obama's remarks was so strong that he was subsequently forced to apologize for them.[23]

The political blogging A-list has also had a direct impact on recent election campaigns. The support of Ned Lamont among several top liberal bloggers, notably Jane Hamsher of *Firedoglake*, is widely credited with helping him win over Senator Joseph Lieberman (D-CT) during the 2006 Democratic senatorial primaries, although Lieberman defeated Lamont during the general election later that year while running as an Independent. More generally, the political mobilization and fundraising efforts of top liberal bloggers is widely credited with ensuring the Democratic takeover of Congress in 2006, making possible a number of crucial wins, including those in Montana, Ohio and Virginia.[24]

The Political Establishment Takes Notice

The considerable power of the top political bloggers hasn't gone unnoticed by the political establishment which has begun to treat them as legitimate journalists in their own right and employ them as campaign consultants. In 2004, and again in 2008, dozens of top liberal and conservative bloggers were granted press passes, alongside their mainstream journalism counterparts, to cover the Democratic and Republican National Conventions. These bloggers are now regularly issued press passes to White House press conferences, and space is made available to them in the press galleries of Congress and local state legislatures. In some instances, they have even been granted special press status. The White House, presidential candidates, members of Congress, governors, and mayors have all convened press conferences and engaged in conference calls attended exclusively by top political bloggers.[25]

Major political figures have begun to meet with the political blogging A-list on its own turf. In 2007, all of the Democratic presidential candidates attended and addressed the Yearly Kos Convention in Chicago, a gathering of more than 1,400 top liberal bloggers, leading one observer to refer to the event as the "Democrats' other national convention."[26]

Political candidates for office have also begun to use top political bloggers as campaign consultants. During the 2008 presidential election, several of the candidates, including Barack Obama, Hillary Clinton, John McCain, and Mitt Romney, hired political bloggers to advise them on how to create productive relationships with the political blogosphere, and did so as early in the election as other types of campaign consultants.[27]

Both the Democratic and Republican parties have held strategy sessions with top political bloggers. The Democratic Party organized a series of meetings where liberal bloggers would advise local press secretaries on how to cultivate relationships with the political blogosphere, and the Republican Party brought local party aids to Capitol Hill to meet with conservative bloggers.[28]

The Heritage Foundation, a major conservative think tank, hosts a weekly meeting in which top conservative bloggers discuss politics with Republican politicians and conservative journalists. Similarly, prominent Democratic politicians, including President Obama and former President Clinton, have met privately with top liberal bloggers on several occasions. As Obama put it, "If you take these blogs seriously, they'll take you seriously."[29]

Finally, and perhaps most tellingly, the political blogging A-list has become so powerful that it has compelled major political figures to join them as guest-bloggers. Among the many politicians who've guest-blogged at top blogs are President Barack Obama, Secretary of State Hillary Clinton, and former House Speaker Nancy Pelosi.[30]

How to Become a Successful Political Blogger

Having read about the stature and influence of the political blogging A-list, it may seem impossible for an ordinary political blogger to break through the mass of bloggers out there and have his or her own voice heard. But it's not only possible; there is much one can do to make it happen.

In the chapters to follow, 20 of the world's top political bloggers, including Arianna Huffington of *The Huffington Post*, the most widely read political blog, explain what they've done to become so successful, and what others can do to emulate their success. The chapters are organized in order of the bloggers' overall daily readership, from highest to lowest, beginning with Arianna Huffington herself. These bloggers aren't only part of the political blogging A-list, they represent the entire political spectrum — from the far-left to the far-right — making their insights applicable to people of all political persuasions. Their advice should be of value to you regardless of whether you recently started blogging, you've been blogging for some time, or you've merely toyed with the idea of creating a blog.

Half of these bloggers had only limited journalistic experience and no high-powered political contacts when they first started blogging. They worked as actors, film producers, investment bankers, models, and record company owners, among many other professions. This reinforces a point that the bloggers repeatedly stressed to me: passion, determination, and sheer hard work are three of the keys to any successful political blog.

During the course of our conversations, these bloggers touched upon many more topics than what makes for a successful political blogger. They also discussed what inspired them to start blogging in the first place; what their overarching goals are and what they do to further those goals; and recounted personal anecdotes about their blogging experiences that they've never revealed before. So, even if you've no intention of starting your own blog, but are among the millions of people who enjoy reading political blogs every day, I'm confident that you'll discover much new and exciting information about some of your favorite bloggers.

1
Arianna Huffington

When Al Gore famously referred to Oprah Winfrey as a "one-woman media empire," he could just as well have been talking about another prominent media personality: Arianna Huffington, the charismatic co-founder and Editor-in-Chief of the liberal *Huffington Post*, the number-one political blog in the world. *Forbes Magazine* has ranked Huffington one of the "Most Influential Women in Media," and *The Observer* of England has named *The Huffington Post* the "Most Powerful Blog in the World." The site has more than 30 million monthly readers and is the most linked-to blog on the Internet. In February, 2011, *The Huffington Post* was acquired by *AOL* for $315 million, making Huffington President and Editor-in-Chief of the newly created *Huffington Post Media Group*.

Born in Athens, Greece and the former wife of Texas oil millionaire Michael Huffington, Huffington has had a storied career as a blogger, author, columnist, and political activist. The author of more than a dozen books, including two best-selling biographies of Maria Callas and Pablo Picasso, she's a nationally syndicated columnist as well as co-host of *Left, Right & Center*, public radio's popular political roundtable program. Huffington also heads The Detroit Project, a public interest group lobbying automakers to produce cars running on alternative fuels. She teamed up with New York University professor Jay Rosen to create a citizen-based online news organization called *OffTheBus*, which presents ordinary people with opportunities to report on presidential elections.

Together with Kenneth Lerer, a media executive, and Jonah Peretti, an Internet entrepreneur, Huffington founded *The Huffington Post* in May 2005. From its inception, with half a dozen site administrators and about 500 bloggers, *The Huffington Post* has become a major news operation with 70 site administrators and more than 3,000 bloggers. Since 2008, several local versions of the site have been launched, including *HuffPost Chicago*, *HuffPost Denver*, *HuffPost Los Angeles*, and *HuffPost New York*.

Besides featuring original news reporting and links to stories in the mainstream news media, much of the political content is written by Huffington herself, a core group of contributors, and thousands of other bloggers, including prominent politicians, celebrities, and journalists such as Barack Obama, Hillary Clinton, Robert Redford, Alec Baldwin, Norman Mailer, and Michael Moore. More than one million comments are posted on the site each month.

The Huffington Post is much more than the largest aggregated political blog in the world. It is, as Huffington prefers to call it, a full-fledged "Internet newspaper" and a "one-stop shop" for news, commentary, and discussion. About a year and a half into the launch, she started to add various non-political sections to the site, including "business," "entertainment," "media," "sports," and "style." Nevertheless, the goal remains the same: to provide a space for liberal political news reporting, commentary, and discussion. Huffington wants people to come to *The Huffington Post* through various means, whether it's the entertainment section or the media section, and then, hopefully, also discover the excitement of politics.

When did you start blogging?

I started blogging when I created a site called *AriannaOnline.com* where I'd write about my books and columns. I also used it to launch different crusades, like A Partnership for a Poll Free America, which was against the prevalence of polling in our culture, and The Detroit Project, which was about trying to lessen our dependence on foreign oil and getting Detroit to wake up before it was too late which, obviously, it was.

I fell in love with the online conversations that ensued, so one of the main reasons why I created *The Huffington Post* was that I felt an important conversation was moving online. Yet, I thought that some of the most important voices of our time weren't online, and that they wouldn't be online unless a platform was created that would make it easy for them.

The first person I invited to blog for me was the historian Arthur Schlesinger. I remember him saying, "What's a blog?" He invited me to lunch in New York to explain it to him, and the bottom line was that he barely typed. So he'd actually fax me his postings. My point is that I wanted the voices out there however way I got them.

I also wanted to make it a one-stop shop, with the most important news and a very vibrant discussion. Creating community was always a big part of it. That's why, from very early on, the comments were always moderated in real time.

**Aside from Arthur Schlesinger, how many bloggers
did you invite to join you in the very beginning?**

I remember that we started with about 500 bloggers. Aside from my own writings, I invited all my friends as well as people — some known, some unknown — who I wanted to be part of the site. We'd a very small team of half a dozen administrators. We knew what we wanted to create, but we didn't really know how long it would take or whether we'd succeed.

What was the biggest challenge you faced when you first started out?

Moderating the comments was a big challenge, because we wanted to maintain a space where people could comment in real time. But, at the same time, we wanted to be careful to avoid the kind of vile attacks that tend to come when people hide behind their anonymity.

What do you do yourself on a typical day?

When I first started the site, I was blogging every day. After two years, I started blogging three times a week, sometimes four times a week. Part of the reason was that, as we were expanding, there was so much work to do with editing the site. So it's very hard for me to describe a typical day. Of course, there are some things I do on a regular basis, like the Monday call with our political editors and reporters where we establish the issues for the week.

Beyond that it's really just constant work. Even when I'm travelling, I'm on my BlackBerry or on my iPhone checking the site, talking to our editors. And I love it. It's been a great joy to see the site grow and also to never have the sense that *this* is *The Huffington Post*. *The Huffington Post* is always a work in progress.

**Aside from hosting several hundred blogs each day, the site features
news and opinion columns as well as coverage of various
non-political topics. How do you view the site?**

We see ourselves as an Internet newspaper. So it's a combination of news, opinion and community. And, about a year and a half after we launched, we started preparing for new sections that weren't political in nature. Right now more than half of our traffic doesn't come from politics.

Do you see *The Huffington Post* as an alternative to traditional news media?

For me, it's not about either/or. I never saw it that way. I've always seen *The Huffington Post* as co-existing with traditional media. I've always seen the future as a hybrid future.

By that I mean the best of the traditional media, in terms of accuracy, fairness, and transparency, and the best of the new media, in terms of immediacy, interactivity, and community. That has always been the goal. And we're increasingly seeing the traditional media doing a fantastic job online. Both the *New York Times* and the *Washington Post* have great sites.

We launched *The Huffington Post's* investigative arm because we see the contraction in the newspaper business and the real need for more investigative journalism.

Who are you trying to reach with the site?

We talk about reaching as many people as possible rather than reaching any particular group. One of the reasons we've multiple sections, including non-political ones, is that we want to reach people whose primary passion in life might not be politics. We want people to come to *The Huffington Post* through various means, whether it's the entertainment section or the media section, and then, hopefully, also discover politics.

Why do you think you've been able to attract and retain so many readers?

Our readers tell us that they consider *The Huffington Post* essential. A lot of them use the term addiction, saying that it's addictive. Part of it, I think, is that we're broad and present the news with our own attitude. We've about 200 original blogs a day on top of all the reported pieces.

And, during the Iran uprising, we showed what we can do by covering a big news story using all the new media, including *Twitter* and *Facebook* and video cameras.

You mentioned earlier that you try to operate the site in terms of the guiding journalistic principles of accuracy, fairness, transparency, immediacy, and interactivity. What else is important to you?

It's important to me, in the stories we choose to feature, that facts are sacred and that we've a clear editorial stance. It's really a combination of both. For instance, in the health-care debate, we tracked from the very beginning what was happening both behind the scenes and in Congress and the White House. We'd an exclusive in posting a memo between the White House and Pharma about their negotiations that led to Pharma's decision not to go against the legislation in exchange for them committing not to have Medicare negotiate for lower prices.

This is an example of how we've stayed with that topic. We'd our reporters write about the memo, which had been denied but leaked to us, in the context of the larger health-care debate. Similarly, we don't have any partisan allegiances, so we've written a lot of things that are critical of the Obama administration and we also welcome diverse voices from others who might not agree with us.

If you were to sum it up, why do you think *The Huffington Post* has been so successful? After all, it's the highest-ranked political blog in the world.

I think we've tapped into this particular moment in terms of how people like to consume their news. People can come to *The Huffington Post* and have everything available at their fingertips, including the nitty-gritty details of the bank bailout or the health care debate.

What advice do you have for people who want to give political blogging a try themselves?

A lot depends on how much time you've at your disposal. If you don't have a lot of time, it can be hard to populate it enough to keep people coming back. It's essential, online, that you've fresh content. Otherwise, people will stop coming. If you only have a little time, it'd be more advantageous to go to a platform like *The Huffington Post* which already has millions of users. That'll give you a very big platform right away.

If, on the other hand, you want to make blogging your living, it'd be good to identify your value-added. What is your unique contribution? And it's good to do some original reporting and developing the stories. Finally, you need to learn how to sustain it, which is done through advertising.

What is the most common mistake you've noticed that less experienced political bloggers tend to make?

One of the most common mistakes is to try to be all things at once, because the key to breaking through online is to have a distinct point of view, a distinct voice, and to offer something unique. And then to build on it. Once you're established, you can build on it and expand, which is what we did with *The Huffington Post*. We first developed our political brand and then kept expanding beyond it.

How, in your opinion, has the political blogosphere evolved over time?

I think the political blogosphere has become very rich. We've a great multiplicity of voices. To me, one of the most promising developments in the political blogosphere has been how Joshua Marshall used *Talking Point Memo*'s community of citizen journalists to break stories like the attorney general story.

**So the work of citizen journalists is becoming
increasingly more important?**

Exactly, and especially in the way news is broken and covered. One of the distinct features of online journalism is what I'd call the obsessive-compulsive nature of it, that you stay with a story and continuously develop it. That's something which is very different from print journalism where you very often have a big blogbasher story. But, then again, big blogbasher stories often die on the front pages of major newspapers.

2
Taegan Goddard

Taegan Goddard's *Political Wire* has a special place in the political blogosphere. Operating much like a traditional wire service, it's the site to which thousands of political insiders – Members of Congress and their staff, political consultants and pollsters, lobbyists, journalists, and political bloggers - go several times a day to get news, analysis, and commentary on the latest political developments that drive political debate in the U.S. Goddard accomplishes this feat by summarizing the reporting of hundreds of mainstream news media outlets, alternative news providers, and other political blogs.

Equally impressive, *Political Wire* is lauded by top liberal and conservative bloggers alike. Arianna Huffington of the liberal *Huffington Post* describes it as "an addictive blog habit you don't want to kick." Glenn Reynolds of the conservative *Instapundit* calls it "one of the absolute must-read sites in the blogosphere." *Political Wire* has also been praised by prominent independent political analysts such as Charlie Cook of *The Cook Political Report* and Stuart Rothenberg of *The Rothenberg Political Report*. *PC Magazine* has named it one of the 20 best political web sites in the world.

Political Wire, a direct descendant of an earlier site called *Political Insider*, dates back to 1997 when Goddard, after having co-authored a highly regarded political management book, decided to pursue his passion for politics on the Internet. The inspiration was a column called the *Washington Wire* which used to run on Fridays on the front page of the *Wall Street Journal*. It contained insider political reporting that, for one reason or another, didn't make it into any of the other published stories that week. Goddard decided to replicate that concept on *Political Wire*, but with a broader geographical focus than on Washington, D.C. and more broadly focused on politics in general.

Prior to launching *Political Wire*, Goddard served as Policy Advisor to the U.S. Senate Committee on Banking, Housing and Urban Affairs and

Connecticut Governor Lowell Weicker. He also spent more than a decade as Managing Director and Chief Operating Officer of Oppenheimer Capital and PIMCO Equity Advisors, both prominent investment firms in New York City.

In addition to blogging, Goddard has written many essays on politics and public policy, which have appeared in dozens of newspapers across the U.S., including the *Boston Globe, Chicago Tribune, San Francisco Chronicle, USA Today*, and the *Washington Post*.

#####

When did you conceive *Political Wire*?

I conceived it more than a dozen years ago, in 1997, when I'd just finished writing a book. I asked myself what I should do next and thought I'd do something on the Internet. I basically tried to replicate something I'd done by email, namely to share some of the latest tidbits about what was happening in politics around the country.

The inspiration for it, really, was a column that used to run on Fridays in the *Wall Street Journal* called the *Washington Wire*. It was a terrific column, going back to when I was in college. I used to love waiting for Friday's *Wall Street Journal* and getting this column, which came out of their Washington, D.C. Bureau. It featured all of these very interesting tidbits, things that may not have made the stories they published over the last week.

But it was interesting reporting detail. It was a lot of the inside baseball of all politics in Washington. What I tried to do with *Political Wire* was to create a similar thing, but be more broadly focused than on Washington and be more broadly focused on politics in general. I think that a lot of the interesting stories that political junkies like go across all levels of government. There are many interesting stories that are happening at local and state-level politics as well as at the federal level.

Another way to look at it is to go back a dozen years. Most newspapers, at the time, were putting their newspapers online in much the same format as their paper versions. So you'd have a national section, a metro section, a business page, a sports page, and a weather page. But there was never a politics section or a politics page.

I always thought that that was something missing from the newspaper. The only thing I had at the time was that column in the *Wall Street Journal* on Fridays, the *Washington Wire*. So *Political Wire* was really trying to serve a need that wasn't met. It's one of the longest-running political blogs out there. Actually, it was launched before blogs were even called blogs.

So it started off as a passion for politics, a hobby, and then it grew and developed into something much, much more.

Did you experience any particular challenges when you first started out?

The biggest challenge, initially, was the technology behind putting up the site. I used some of the very earliest blog software packages. The first one I used was called *Gray Matter*, which I doubt even exists today.

But it was very exciting for me. When I originally started the site, it was all hand-coded, and every single day I'd to put up the page anew. Then I moved to *Moveable Type*, followed by *Word Press*, and those have made it much easier to blog. I wish I'd have had those a dozen years ago. So technology was the biggest challenge.

You mentioned that you launched *Political Wire* to serve a need that wasn't met at the time. What has kept you going all these years?

The interesting thing is that it's something I'd probably do anyway. I think the key to any successful blog is that the person running it has a complete passion for it. I think that that's why *Political Wire* has become so popular over the years, because it's very clear that this is something that really comes naturally to me. I never tire of it. I've been doing it for over a dozen years, and I've never once tired of it.

The other thing that truly keeps you going is the feedback, that you become part of a much broader conversation on the Internet. In the early years, the feedback was almost entirely by email. Obviously, in more recent years, the feedback comes via *Facebook* and *Twitter* as well as other blogs and websites. People begin to start posting their own reactions to things I've said. *Political Wire* has become, I think, part of the political eco-system on the Internet. It's part of that conversation.

There are literally thousands of people who start their day, every day, with the site. And many of those people have all the mechanisms of the Internet available for letting their own feelings and opinions be known, as well as for disseminating interesting perspectives and interesting bits of news. So *Political Wire* is really part of a much broader conversation and, I think, actually helps support it. I enjoy that. I enjoy being part of that much broader conversation. And I really think that, if *Political Wire* was to go away, it'd be missed.

Political Wire is one of the largest aggregator sites.
How do you go about collecting all that material?

That's another thing that has changed over the years. In the early years, I was probably one of the first people to use RSS feeds, and I'd even create RSS feeds for sites that didn't have them yet. But, now, almost every news site has a RSS feed. That's a great and easy way to keep track of dozens of potential sources of interesting news. So, on a very practical basis, one of the first things I do is scan the news.

There's also this feedback mechanism which started and continues with email, but now also includes *Twitter*. Tweets have become a fascinating way of learning what other people find interesting, and it's also very much happening in real time. So if something is happening, you'll know even before the *Associated Press, Reuters*, or any of the other news wires out there.

You can pretty much find out what's going on through *Twitter*. You begin to get a sense of what's happening, what's important, what reactions are to various events. And you can begin to actually write about them before any of the traditional news sources are reporting on them.

Who do you do it for?

I do it for the same people who, going back a dozen years, always wanted that political page. So, in a practical sense, it's for people who're very similar to me, who like politics to the same degree that I do and also enjoy it almost as a game. While some people might read the sports page first every day, there's a whole group of people who read *Political Wire* first every day, because that's something that gets them going in the morning.

Those people, I find, are professionally employed in politics or public affairs. They work either in political offices or on campaigns, or are elected and appointed officials themselves. In many cases they're journalists who cover politics and, obviously, there are also the political junkies out there who just find it interesting.

Do you do anything in particular to retain those readers over time?

I've been fortunate that the site has been around so long that there's a built-in base of people who talk about it and who pass it along through word of mouth or email. I think the key to making sure that you've a steady amount of traffic is simply to remain true to the mission of the site. If your passion for politics shows through, and you keep putting up good quality content, people will keep coming back.

I've found over the years that, during each election cycle, I get a new burst of readers as politics becomes more interesting to a greater number of people. After each cycle is over, traffic diminishes a bit, but it always levels out at a higher level than in the previous cycle. So, every two years that passes, it grows. Word of mouth is the key thing, and the way to get good word of mouth is to make sure that you put up good content.

What, in your opinion, is the most salient feature of an outstanding political blog?

The number one requirement is that there's a person whose personality and whose passion comes through on the site. Blogs are really one-person sites. While you can have blogs hosted by larger sites, and they can become popular, the blog itself has to be identified with one person. There are group blogs that succeed, but the ones that do have single individuals who rise above the rest of the contributors.

I think that personality really does matter. And when I say personality, I mean that people can be very passionate or activist in their viewpoints and take various sides on various issues. In the case of *Political Wire*, it's not so much about being an activist or about taking sides, but it's about showing this passion for politics that's shared by Republicans, Democrats and Independents alike.

So it's a different type of passion, but I think that that same passion and my personality come through. Ultimately, that's what's important, because people end up trusting the person. You could read the *New York Times*, and you could trust the institution for giving you the right type of news. But, in the case of a blog, there's really no institution as much as there's a person. And, as you begin to read, as you begin to investigate, you end up having more confidence in that person and that blog over time.

What advice would you give people who want to launch a political blog themselves?

I'd tell them that passion is the most important thing, because you never want to get bored. You need to realize that, if you're committing to something, if you want to build a readership, it has to be a daily thing. And if you get tired of it quickly, or you think you're going to get tired of it in a few months, it's probably not worth the effort.

The other thing, if you're just starting out, is to understand the market. Know who else is out there. Understand if what you're creating is new or has a different twist than things that are already out there. It's pretty hard to start something up and be successful if you don't know all of the competitors. I use that term loosely, because I don't think blogs are competitors in the same sense that media companies have been. You can have hundreds of blogs, and they'll all kind of work together and feed into each other.

Do you have any other, more specific advice for aspiring political bloggers?

In terms of your writing style, you need to be yourself. Trying to be someone else, trying to take on a different voice, or trying to be controversial where there's no controversy or you don't feel it, never works.

There are some very good smaller sites out there where you'd never think any would be. You'd never think that that was a topic big enough that it'd interest somebody. But then you find somebody who just has a tremendous passion and an interesting personality, and it all comes through and makes for a very enjoyable read.

What's the biggest mistake that less experienced political bloggers tend to make?

The biggest mistake newly established bloggers make is that they start out their site on an established blogging platform, like *Blogger* or *Word Press*. That makes it very easy to get it up and running, but they end up getting wedded to a URL that's hosted. It also makes you seem less serious and less important right off the bat. While you may have some very good content, a lot of people, particularly the more sophisticated bloggers out there, won't take you as seriously as if you had your own domain name. And, obviously, having your own domain name and setting it up, even with one of those hosted systems, is really not that hard. So that's something that everybody, especially if you're really serious about it, should do: get their own domain name.

What trends do you see with respect to the future of political blogging?

Let me answer by talking a bit about what news is. You can refer to news as a stream. There's this constant stream happening in real time, even as we're speaking right now, that you need to be able to figure out. You need to have the right tools and be able to figure out what's important and what's going on. What does it mean? It's happening continuously, so it's an interesting challenge. I think most traditional news organizations have had a hard time with that.

I think that blogs are in a much better position to make sense of that than traditional news organizations. And I think that blogs will look very different in the future, because it won't just be about putting up a webpage. In fact, it'll be less about putting up a webpage than about putting it out there where people can then tap into it in a variety of ways. People aren't just reading these sites in front of a computer. They're reading them on all sorts of devices, all over the place.

The blog, as we think of it today, is essentially a webpage. I think that some of these newer communications technologies, like *Twitter*, are going to change that. Blogs are going to be different and you're not just going to be able to tap into a webpage. There are going to be ways for you to put your thoughts and your analysis out there into what I call the stream of news, and it'll look very different than it does today.

There'll be people who'll access it only on their phones or on their BlackBerries. There'll be people to whom it won't look like a webpage at all. There'll be people who access it on other reading devices. The underlying publishing model will be very different than it is today. I see that as the direction we're going, although I can't tell you what it's going to look like.

3
Jane Hamsher

Many of the world's top political bloggers can trace their rise to blogging stardom back to a particular incident. For Jane Hamsher of the progressive liberal blog *Firedoglake*, the defining moment was her coverage of the 2007 federal perjury trial of I. Lewis ("Scooter") Libby, a Senior Advisor to former Vice President Dick Cheney, who was indicted for his role in the leak of classified information about CIA operative Valerie Plame.

Together with five of her co-bloggers, Hamsher live-blogged the trial directly from the courtroom, after having been granted press passes. It was one of the first federal cases for which independent political bloggers had been given official press credentials alongside mainstream journalists. Online donors to *Firedoglake* helped defray Hamsher's and her co-bloggers' costs of covering the trial; paying for their travel expenses and the renting of the apartment in Washington, D.C. that they shared. Even though no audio or video feed was permitted in the courtroom, their coverage was so exhaustive that many of the major mainstream news organizations depended on it for their own reporting. *Firedoglake* subsequently won the prestigious Koufax Award for "Best Series" in recognition of its trial coverage.

Following the trial, *Firedoglake*, named after Hamsher's favorite pastime of sitting by the fire with her dog watching a *Los Angeles Lakers* game, emerged as one of the largest and most influential progressive liberal blogs. Now, with about a dozen site administrators and more than 20 regular contributors, the site features news reporting, analysis, and commentary on all the pressing political issues of the day; however, *Firedoglake* offers much more than that. The site serves as a means to raise consciousness about, mobilize around, and raise money for various progressive liberal causes. The site also features a section called "FDL Book Salon" in which prominent liberal intellectuals discuss recent books on political topics with the site's readers and the authors themselves. Together with Markos Moulitsas of the liberal blog *Daily Kos*, where she initially started blogging as a diarist, Hamsher also runs a book imprint called "FDL Books." Its first release was a volume about the Valerie Plame / Scooter Libby affair by *Firedoglake* and *Daily Kos* contributor Marcy Wheeler. *Firedoglake* also features a section called "FDL Action" through which millions of dollars have been raised for various progressive liberal candidates and causes, and Hamsher herself is involved with a number of other political action groups, including Accountability Now, Act Blue, and Public Option Please.

Prior to launching *Firedoglake*, in 2004, Hamsher was a successful Hollywood film producer and author, with many well-known movies to her credit. She's best known as the co-producer, with Don Murphy, of the 1994 movie *Natural Born Killers,* written by Quentin Tarantino and directed by Oliver Stone, and as the author of the best-selling book *Killer Instinct*, a memoir about her experiences co-producing the movie.

#####

Why did you start *Firedoglake*?

I started it about seven years ago because I was interested in the whole culture around blogging. I'd been very interested in how Ralph Reed had been able to connect the churches into an existing network, bringing them together in order to create an incredible mass around a group of people who've similar interests.

But there was no liberal answer to that. You couldn't really organize the produce section of *Whole Foods*. Blogging seemed like it could be the liberal answer to that.

Did you start out on your own?

Yes. I started out blogging on *Daily Kos*, and then I just put up my own blog on the free *Blogspot* platform.

When did you start to add contributors?

A few months after things started to get really busy. I was covering the Scooter Libby case, the Valerie Plame situation, and I'd a lot of work to do. So I added people then.

Have you experienced any particular challenges, especially with managing the rapid growth of the site?

Yes. It's hard, because there's no model for it. In large part, we were able to do what we did because the *New York Times* and the *Wall Street Journal* didn't know how to make money on it. So they just kind of abandoned the space. But it's always been a challenge. What are your priorities? Which way do you go? Where do you invest?

So, yes, it's been a challenge from a business standpoint. There's no solid business model for it yet.

Briefly put, what are you trying to accomplish?

We're trying to bring about progressive change. We're trying to create the conditions that make that possible.

So you see *Firedoglake* as a political grassroots effort?

Absolutely. The great thing about blogging is that it's grassroots. It goes directly to the grassroots. It allows the grassroots to organize themselves without the need for intermediaries who're capable of being swayed by particular interests.

How do you decide what to blog about on any given day?

Part of it is what your audience wants you to cover, what they're interested in, and part of it is what you think you could bring something special to.

So you get actual requests from your readers?

Yes. Blogging, as you know, is a two-way street. It's very different from doing a newspaper article. Readers show up in your comments. They tell you what they think. They tell you what they want. They talk about the things they're interested in. You can sort of channel the flow of conversation, but you can't control it.

On that note, who're your readers?

Our readers tend to be between the ages of 40 and 60. They make between $100,000 and $150,000 a year. They're approximately 68% male and 32% female, and about 40% have done post-graduate work. They're the people who vote. They're the people who give money to political campaigns. They're politically knowledgeable.

That's a fairly educated and affluent audience?

That's just who's online. It tends to be people who during the day at work are on computers. It's a cross-section of that world.

What do you do to attract and retain those readers?

We try to be responsive to what our readers want us to cover, what their values are. But we also try to lead when we think that something is important. We'll keep talking about it whether it's driving traffic or not.

For instance, labor is one of those issues that never really had a natural constituency in the political blogosphere, but we were committed to covering it over time. So when the Employee Free Choice Act battle came up, our audience was ready for it. They knew what the stakes were and what was going on. And they were very engaged in that fight.

A lot of organizations online sort of float from outrage of the minute to outrage of the minute. Even though you have to address a story that people are talking about, you can still continue to feed long-term awareness of a particular situation. And when it comes around in the news, you can create a movement around it.

On that note, what do you see as the defining features of a high-quality political blog?

The ability to use the medium to advance the narrative past the superficial coverage that the mainstream media often devote to something. People talk about bloggers as being moment-to-moment and not doing any real research, but that's not true. The best blogs carry institutional memory. They act as repositories for documents. People know their own particular subject really, really well.

What do you do to distinguish *Firedoglake* in the political blogosphere more generally?

We try to empower people at the grassroots level to be able to bring about political change. So we're more activist-oriented than many other blogs. But we're also very much into creating a model for activism that utilizes what the Internet can do well and breaking out of the past's model that hasn't been very successful.

Could you elaborate on that?

Sure. In the past, especially in the U.S., the activist model was sort of the Ralph Nader model of the 1970s where a group of elites formed a consensus and then Congress was supposed to respond. It just hasn't worked for 40 years.

While the lobbyists were working very effectively behind the scenes to advance their own interests, liberal groups and constituencies were paralyzed by a variety of limitations. How do we overcome those limitations? By fighting the battle where it's being fought, using the strength of the Internet. That's what we try to do.

Why do you think *Firedoglake* has been so successful?

Because we demonstrated early on with our coverage of the Scooter Libby trial what it is people want from blogs. And when that story came into the news, they wanted a place where they could go and read about it, whatever happened that minute. So we were very careful about making sure that we addressed that desire. But once you have people's eyeballs, you have to work to keep them.

On that note, if you were to hold up an example of a successful political blogger to people who want to launch a political blog themselves, who'd that be?

Nate Silver. He's the best example. He blogged at *Daily Kos* and managed to build up an audience there so he was able to transfer to his own site, *FiveThirtyEight*. He'd a particular skill that others didn't have, and he applied it at the time of the 2008 presidential election. The statistics that he writes about inform the news in a very compelling way.

So he managed to build an audience for himself. But had he just started his own site, he probably wouldn't have gotten many links. You have to create awareness within existing structures before you start your own site.

So you'd encourage people to start blogging at a more established site before they venture out on their own?

Yes, that'd be my advice.

Would it make any difference, if you want to start your own site, whether you do it on your own or together with one or more like-minded individuals?

No, because you're searching for an audience. You're not searching for co-bloggers.

So you need a pre-existing audience?

Yes. Even I started out at *Daily Kos* many years ago. Then I went to other people's sites, became friends with them, and they'd link to me. You really have to work yourself into the culture. It's like moving into a new neighborhood.

What mistakes have you noticed that less experienced political bloggers typically make?

Usually, the mistake is that they tend to be generalists. It's very hard to compete as a generalist. Look at Arianna Huffington or Marcos Moulitsas who're really at the top of the game. These people can be generalists if they want to, although even they tend to specialize.

You have to do something special. You have to do something unique. You have to find a niche and fill it. We do a lot of work with people who do local blog coverage, which we try and network into the community. It may just be what's in your own backyard. If nobody's covering it, you can really control what the story is around it.

So you'd recommend people to start out blogging about a very particular, even local, issue?

Yes.

And that could be?

It all depends on what you do. If you're covering a local issue, you may not want to go with a national blog but with a state blog, like *MyLeftNutmeg* does with Connecticut politics. If you want to cover Connecticut politics, start out at *MyLeftNutmeg*. It's a group blog.

Briefly put, how has the political blogosphere changed since you became involved with it?

A lot of our development has more to do with the political landscape than it does with us. At the same time that we're maturing, and the online audience is maturing, we've exited the shouting phase of President Bush, and we've entered the sausage-making phase of President Obama. So we've got to figure out as writers and activists how to talk about making policy as opposed to just expressing our outrage over things we don't like.

4
Eric Olsen

Blogcritics, which Eric Olsen founded in 2002 together with Phillip Winn, the site's Technical Director — can best be described as an anomaly in the higher echelons of the political blogosphere. Unlike other top political blogs, which tend to be either liberal, conservative, libertarian, or centrist, *Blogcritics* is officially non-denominational. The site's goal is to serve as an open forum where all political perspectives are treated equally and with respect. By showcasing a variety of political perspectives, Olsen has nurtured a space where bloggers of different political persuasions can and do debate their opinions civilly with others.

Like *The Huffington Post*, *Blogcritics* features a number of topical sections in addition to politics, including "Books," "Culture," "Music," "Sports," and "Television/Film," and relies on more than 3,000 contributing bloggers from all around the world for its coverage. Every week about 350 new postings are added to the archive of more than 100,000 postings, and more than 600,000 comments have been contributed to the site since its inception. But, unlike *The Huffington Post* and many other top political blogs, a team of 20 editors review every posting and comment prior to publication. This is done to ensure that postings are uniformly well-written and informative, and that comments are offered in a spirit of respect for opposing viewpoints.

Blogcritics has won several awards, including the prestigious "Bloggie" award and a "Best Media Blog" award from *Forbes Magazine*. It's an accredited news source for *Google News* and *Yahoo! News*, and its content is syndicated to online editions of newspapers across the U.S.

Like the site that he founded, Olsen, too, has an unusual background. Prior to launching *Blogcritics*, Olsen had a 30-year career as a freelance writer for all kinds of publications, owned and operated a record company, hosted his own radio show, and worked as a music critic and author, having written three books on different music-related topics. Olsen's forays into political blogging began in late 2001 when he was doing research for a book on the relationship between the 9/11 terrorist attacks and the Internet. Fascinated by the conversations that took place online, and especially in the bourgeoning political blogosphere, Olsen decided to create a place where all the bloggers could put the material that didn't necessarily fit on their own home sites.

#####

Could you begin by recounting your personal and professional road to blogging?

Sure. I'm an author. I'd three books on music-related topics published in the 1990s. I've been a freelance writer for all kinds of publications, local, regional and national, going back to about 1980— a long time. So I've an extensive writing background.

I was researching a book on the relationship between 9/11 and the Internet, because I was fascinated by what appeared to be the first time that a major, real-world event was directly impacted by the Internet. Because the cell phone towers were out, people, especially in Manhattan, were literally communicating in real time via the Internet, letting their families know that they were alive, where they were, and so on.

Of course, you also had the immediate reaction to the event. You had millions of people worldwide, especially in the U.S., needing an outlet for all the feelings that they were having, in addition to a need for real-time information. The message boards were going crazy. The Internet just kind of exploded in terms of usage.

My co-author and I found the reality of it so fascinating that we were doing all kinds of research all over the Internet. And, in doing so, I started running into these things called blogs that I'd never heard of before. This was late 2001 and early 2002. I didn't know what they were but was fascinated by the idea, especially when I came across Andrew Sullivan's site, *The Daily Dish*. I'd known him, although not in person, as the Editor of *The New Republic* in the 1990s. So I knew who he was. I also knew what he did, how he thought. When I saw his site, I thought to myself, "Oh, okay. This can be a professional, but independent, journalistic approach to the world."

I saw that he was taking it very seriously, putting a lot of time and effort into it. He was posting daily, usually multiple times a day, and basically using it as an outlet for his columns, with less formal presentation and development of his ideas. I thought that was really fascinating.

The thing that had always frustrated me, basically since the day I first started freelance writing, was the amount of time and effort that you have to put into marketing your ideas. You can put as much time and effort into that as you can into researching and writing the story itself. It'd always struck me as an incredible waste of time, incredible waste of effort, even humiliating. So, I thought, this is ideal. This is a place where I can place my writing. I can write about serious matters. Because that was certainly a very serious time. People were thinking very serious thoughts.

So I did a lot of research, trying to understand what was going on in the world, with millions of people suddenly waking up from a daze and becoming very, very tuned in.

I thought it was tremendous. So I started writing to Andrew Sullivan, just kind of picking his brain, asking him how all of this worked. He was very responsive and very encouraging. Eventually, after a few weeks I suppose, he just said, "Dude, quit bugging me. Start your own site." So I responded, "Okay, I guess I will."

I started a site with two other people. We were all record producers. I've put out a couple of albums of electronic music. One of my partners was much more tech savvy than I was. I didn't have any concept at all of HTML, or anything else relating to the Internet for that matter. So he became our tech guy. We started a site called *Tres Producers* and got a pretty strong response. So I figured why not throw myself into this and see what happens. I'll treat it like a job. I was writing a lot, posting a lot, because I'd all this writing background.

My background is pretty varied. I've written professionally on almost every aspect of popular culture, music, TV, and film. But I've also written quite a bit about politics. I was a Political Science and Philosophy major in college. So I'd at least the theoretical background.

So I just started writing about all these things. I very quickly realized, as I mentioned earlier, that this was a very serious time. People were really worried about what was going on. Nothing was really resolved yet. You still had the anthrax scare hanging over everyone's head. No one knew what was going to happen. You'd war pending and all kinds of very intense things.

I learned very quickly from communicating with all kinds of bloggers that it was all about linking and helping each other out and finding kindred spirits, not necessarily in the sense of people who agree with you but who're interested in expressing themselves as well as being open-minded.

I got to know probably half of the top 50 bloggers in the English language in a matter of months. It wasn't that hard, because I was applying myself. And, at the time, there weren't that many people. It was still a very new thing.

The war bloggers were a new phenomenon. The tech bloggers, who were the ones that started the whole thing in the first place back in the 1990s, felt somewhat threatened by them and all the attention they were getting. It was interesting to follow.

Within a few months, in February of 2002, I started my site. I got a lot of response, wrote a lot, and took it pretty seriously. I realized that many bloggers were quite eclectic in their interests. So, I thought to myself, what about coming up with a place where all these bloggers could put the material that didn't necessarily fit on their home sites. That was the idea. That was the germ for *Blogcritics*. It kind of boggles my mind now. I started my site in February. By August we had *Blogcritics*.

Aside from politics, *Blogcritics* features a number of other topics. Could you talk about your experiences with the political bloggers relative to the other bloggers?

That's a very good question because to this day, more than nine years later, there's still a perceived barrier between the politics section, which gets the great majority of the site's comments and has some of the most committed bloggers and readers, and the other sections.

One of the benefits for the bloggers is simply getting vastly more exposure and visibility than they'd get on their own sites and having many, many more readers. They're being recognized and getting indexed in *Google News*. It's people who feel the need to express themselves on political matters and who like and appreciate the heightened attention and exposure that they get from the site.

We found that the majority of the people who write about politics don't write anywhere else. So we've key people who've been around a long time. They tend to be very independent. They tend to be out for themselves in terms of getting exposure.

You've talked about the motivation of your political bloggers. What's your own motivation for having a politics section on the site?

When we first started out, during the first couple of weeks, we didn't have a politics section. But I quickly realized that it's really important to have political stories. It was a key part of what was going on in the blogosphere. And a number of other bloggers said, "We'd like to do that. We'd like to be able to put those stories there."

So, ultimately, it really was that simple and that selfish. I wanted to be able to blog about politics myself. So, I said, "Okay. We're going to have a politics section."

Do you try to feature certain political positions, or do you try to create a space for various political views?

We're non-denominational. I've always seen a need for a place that's essentially an open forum where all perspectives are treated equally and with respect. There's no Litmus test of political affiliation or political ideas.

And, as I'm sure you know, there are virtually no other sites where you've a cross-section of political ideas and opinions, where the whole political spectrum is open and welcome.

We feel very strongly that there's a need for a place that's a positive and open forum, where people can express their points of view and have those points of view challenged, often strongly, but in an open and positive manner.

We try to enforce a comment policy of no personal attacks. We try to keep it as open as possible and amenable to conversation. We don't want to chase people off. So the purpose is to have an open forum where people can express themselves well and get out and test their ideas outside of the echo chamber.

Who're you trying to reach with *Blogcritics*?

We're trying to reach a well-educated, politically astute, and active audience. There's a certain assumption of knowledge in a lot of our stories, especially because they're opinion pieces.

So, although what we're looking for ideally is a self-contained essay with a beginning, a middle, and an end, there's the assumption that people know what's going on, what the main variables are as far as what's going on in the news.

We're working from an assumption of highly educated and politically energized readers. And the kind of people we're looking for, again, are those who wish to escape the echo chamber.

You can go to any number of political sites and it's fairly obvious fairly quickly what their agenda is. And the people who write and comment there are typically people who're drawn to that point of view.

We're not espousing any particular point of view. We want it to be a place to come to present your ideas well, in a logical, coherent, well-written manner, and see how those ideas stand up to rigorous examination by those who don't necessarily agree with you.

More generally, what makes for an outstanding political blog in your opinion?

In the most basic terms there are four elements: bloggers, editors, commenters, and readers. You need all four.

I especially feel that any well-done site has to have editors. I feel strongly that all stories should be edited prior to publication. Ours are articles with a beginning, a middle, and an end. They're supposed to be self-contained. Certainly, there are links to supporting material and so on. But the reader is supposed to be able to get all the information they need from within the story.

Aside from having editors and trying to create an open and welcoming space for political expression and discussion, what else makes *Blogcritics* stand apart in the political blogosphere?

I think our comments section is different in that we try very hard to maintain a balance between a maximum of openness, a maximum of free speech, and an atmosphere where people don't feel threatened and personally attacked, where they feel that their perspectives are respected.

We've two comments editors, in addition to our story editors. I think they do a remarkable job of maintaining that balance between free speech and a welcoming environment, where people of differing opinions can have their ideas challenged but in a respectful manner.

Why do you think *Blogcritics* has been so successful?

Ultimately, *Blogcritics* is a filtered microcosm of the political blogosphere more generally. So a reader can get a pretty good sense of what the parameters are, what's being discussed, what's important. At any given time, it offers a pretty accurate slice, a fairly accurate cross-section, of the river as the river flows by.

So, ultimately, I think, that's the foundation of our strength. Aside from that, we offer professional, mainstream media writing quality but rising out of individuals and the independence and attitude of the blogosphere.

This is certainly what keeps us going. We reside right at that crux between the mainstream media and the blogosphere and we partake of the best of both.

What advice would you give someone who wants to launch a political blog himself?

If I was to start afresh myself, I think a dual approach would be best. I'd say, first, that you certainly would want to have your own site. You'd want to have it set up in a presentable manner so that people who come to your site will take it seriously. There is any number of platforms where you relatively easily can create a fairly professional site.

If you want to get attention, you for sure have to write a lot. The more the better. But you don't want to just blurt out anything and everything. It's also important to define yourself, somehow, in some way. How do you establish yourself as different? How do you find your niche? You have to be really self-aware and figure out the parameters of your thinking, your beliefs. What matters to you? What's your purview? What are your areas of interest?

At the same time, I'd definitely also go to various group blogs. There are a number of sites where you can put your material for a larger audience and interact on that level. The more of those you participate in, the better off you'll be. But, at some point, you need to narrow it down and try to figure out which ones are the best for you. And that's not necessarily just a matter of traffic. It may just be where you feel most comfortable, where you feel most challenged, where you feel you're reaching people who're important to you for whatever reason.

So, if I was starting out from scratch tomorrow, I'd start my own site, but I'd also go to a number of group blogs and start working in that mode.

Are there certain mistakes that less experienced political bloggers are especially prone to make?

Let me answer by giving you an example. We'd a woman who wrote a very passionate and heart-felt political story about being a veteran, a very pro-American, very right-down-the-middle conservative story.

It received 300-400 comments almost right away and is still getting comments. Yet, she was appalled that anyone would dare criticize her opinion. She felt that she controlled that space and that it should be her right to allow whatever comments she wanted or not wanted on her story.

It took a lot of effort on my part. I finally had to call her on the phone, because she was losing her mind, and explain to her that it's like having a child. Once you send that story into the world, once that story is published, you don't control it anymore. It becomes the purview of the readers and the commenters.

We've no rules about comments having to be on topic. We've no rules about comments having to be nice. About the only thing we have is the rule that you can't engage in personal attacks and, more generally, that people treat each other with respect. But surprise. That's not always followed.

So being open to criticism is very important?

Yes, and you have to have thick skin. You can't control a thread once it's begun. It takes on a life of its own. In fact, it's not your place to control it. Aside from that, she should have been happy that so many people were interested in what she'd to say and participated in that conversation.

If she felt compelled to defend her point of view, she should have defended her story in the comments. That's fine. But once she's done that, there's really no reason to stick around, because you don't control it.

It was just very graphic that someone brand new to the Internet, who hadn't written for the Internet before, was completely caught off guard. She'd no idea that this could happen when, in fact, it's perfectly normal.

This is something that's not unusual, especially for people who're new to the Internet. In fact, especially some professional, long-time writers feel that they should have control. That's been a problem that a lot of the mainstream media sites have had to adapt to.

A lot of them have taken the comments function away, because they don't want to have to bother to police them. They don't want to bother with all the issues that come up in providing that forum. And, ultimately, they don't like the fact that they can't control it. But if they did control it, it'd take the heart and soul out of it.

Briefly put, where does political blogging stand today?

I think the political blogosphere was greatly re-energized and given a new focus by the Obama campaign, either for or against it. The people who're pro are very pro. The people who're opposed are very opposed. So it really re-energized the political blogosphere and, certainly, his election.

Now, you're essentially defined by either being pro or against Obama and his policies. That focus is very intense. Important issues are being debated right now, so I think that'll continue for a while.

5
Andrew Malcolm

One of the most commonly-held beliefs among online enthusiasts is that old-time print and broadcast journalists resist the brave new world of political blogging at all costs. If there ever was an exception to that "rule," that person would surely be Andrew Malcolm of the *Los Angeles Times'* national politics blog, *Top of the Ticket*.

After a long and distinguished career at the *New York Times* where he served as both a foreign and national correspondent, Assistant National Editor, and national affairs correspondent, Malcolm worked in government and politics for eight years, including two years as former First Lady Laura Bush's Press Secretary. In 2001, Malcolm joined the *Los Angeles Times* where he's been ever since, including five years on the Editorial Board when he was a Pulitzer Prize Finalist in 2004.

When Doug Frantz, one of the Managing Editors, asked Malcolm to design a political blog for the paper in 2007, he didn't, as some might have predicted, resist. To the contrary, Malcolm relished the challenge and drew up the blueprint for a blog that would be "an equal opportunity offender." Even a cursory look at the spirited reactions that Malcolm's postings frequently inspire, both on and off the blog, attests to his success.

For Malcolm, who regularly puts in 15-16 hour work days, the attractions of blogging are many. Increasingly unhappy with the bureaucratic structure of the newsroom, and what he calls "the girdled format of newspaper writing," blogging has given him the freedom to focus on the topics about which he's truly passionate, and to write about them exactly the way he wants. He also enjoys the sheer immediacy of blogging, the fact that readers react almost instantaneously to his postings. To Malcolm, there isn't anything more exciting professionally than seeing readers falling all over themselves electronically to get at his writing.

Malcolm's ability to attract and provoke thousands of readers daily owes much to his innovative and humorous headlines, of which he gives several examples during the interview, as well as to what he calls his "lingerie theory of communication." Likening his writing style to a woman's night gown, he tries not to reveal the full picture at once under the belief that it's what readers can't yet see that makes them intrigued to continue reading. The subtle result is that readers are drawn in to wonder what it is, to continue to look and see more. Indeed, writing a blog post is an exploratory trip for Malcolm himself: It's usually not until about two-thirds of the way through that he realizes how an item is going to end.

#####

What inspired you to start blogging?

In the tenth grade in high school, I decided that I wanted to be a foreign correspondent. My English teacher said, "Well, then you'll want to work for *The New York Times*." So I said, "Ok," and started reading *The New York Times*. Through a long road full of an embarrassing amount of chutzpa, I got a job at *The New York Times* after I finished graduate school in July of 1967.

I worked there until 1993. That's 26 years. I worked in New York, covering the United Nations. I worked in the Chicago Bureau and the San Francisco Bureau. I was in Vietnam and Thailand. Then I went to Tokyo as the Bureau Chief, to Toronto as the Bureau Chief, and finally to Chicago as the Bureau Chief. I became the Assistant National Editor and wrote the "Our Towns" column.

I left in 1993 to accept a challenge from the Governor of Montana to put my mouth where my money had been all those years writing about politics. I worked in politics for eight years and was involved in the 2000 Bush campaign, mainly as Mrs. Bush's Press Secretary. Then I joined the Editorial Board of the *Los Angeles Times* in 2001 and have been here ever since.

A little over four years ago, one of the Managing Editors, Doug Frantz, asked me, "What do you want to do next on this paper?" So I drew up a list, went into his office, and he heard me out. He said, "Well, those ideas are fine. But here's what I'd like you to do."

His idea was better. He said, "Why don't we put your 30 plus years of journalism experience and your eight years of government experience to use for the paper? Why don't you design a politics blog? What kind of a blog should it be, and how should we do it?"

I spent some weeks reading other blogs and came up with a proposal for *Top of the Ticket*, which was basically an equal opportunity offender blog that would blog on anything political from coast-to-coast. It'd be running almost 24 hours a day and suffused with attitude and the unexpected.

I've a son that has been in the online business for many years, so I've sort of watched him as a bystander and realized that one of the main reasons I like to go online is the serendipity of it. You never know what you're going to find. It's like beach combing.

On most of the political blogs, you know exactly what you're going to find. In fact, most readers probably go to them because they're comfortable and very predictable. But I decided that our niche would be to be unpredictable.

Typically, the topics I write about, and certainly the way I write about them, are unpredictable. That seems to have found a market. There are a lot of people who come for that.

I launched the blog in June of 2007 and have had several thousand items and more than 100,000 comments. I passed 33 million readers in less than two years. So the blog did find a market for itself and, surprising to my mind, with a fairly substantial overseas readership, in addition to a broad, national readership. Since I've been on *Twitter*, I've been getting thousands of followers.

How has the experience been so far?

It's been very exciting. I got into journalism, because I wanted to do something different every day, and because I wanted to learn something new every day. And I did early on in my career. But the bureaucracy of the newsroom and the girdled format of newspaper writing limited that. It limited my ability to write, although I didn't know it was going to lead to blogging. But it certainly led to a lot of frustrations. You'd write things and say, "Boy, there's a great paragraph, but it'll never see the light of day." The next morning, of course, it was gone.

So the excitement to me of online journalism is the immediacy, the relationship with readers, which is fairly direct. I love the reality that I can post an item, as I did just now, and in 20 minutes I can see that people are coming.

There were times during the last presidential election when, at the end of the day, I'd do the math and notice that I'd posted an item and 20 minutes later the numbers would start to grow. At the end of the day, I'd figure out that we'd 30 new readers arriving on my blog every second for hours at a time.

If you're a professional storyteller, and dominated "show and tell" time in the sixth grade as I did, there isn't anything more exciting professionally than seeing people falling all over themselves electronically to get at your writing. I can't get enough of it and regularly put in 15–16 hour days.

I love it. The rewards have been great. There's an element of show business to it. I've written 10 non-fiction books, and I'm somewhat older. So I'm perhaps more comfortable than young people would be in allowing a certain voice to come through.

I want readers, if they're new to the blog, to go, "Whoa, who's writing this?" and to look for a byline. If they've been on the blog before, I want them to feel that this item, whatever it's about, has been processed through a very particular mind. They may agree with it, they may disagree with it, but the reality is that they come here to see what that take is. And they can leave their own in the comments.

Have you experienced any particular challenges along the way? Blogging is obviously very different from more conventional journalistic writing.

Yes, and thank God for that. It does differ. It has more freedom. It's more informal.

I've covered political summits, trade talks, and all that stuff for many years. The first political event I ever covered was the 1968 Democratic riot in Chicago. I was standing right there when Mayor Richard Daley was doing the throat-cutting motion at Abraham Ribicoff. So it's been a long time. I've seen a lot of changes.

And although I got along very well in journalism and enjoyed most of it, I'd considerable frustrations with the strict format, and the girdled approach to everything limited the way I did my job. There wasn't much I could do, except to have spicier quotes and to use stronger verbs to tell stories.

When they first approached me about blogging, I said to my son, "My God, how am I ever going to find five or six things to write about every day?" My son responded, "Don't worry. You will." I start every day with half a dozen things. I write half a dozen and, at the end of the day, I've got ten items. The frustration is not having the time or the strength to do them all, because there's so much to write.

The only real challenge, which has been easily overcome by diligence, has been mechanical. It's been learning the coding and how to do certain things. I found that I was technologically challenged.

When I was in government, I was a very proactive communications person. I wasn't sitting by the phone waiting for trouble to happen and somebody to call me for a comment. I was out every day, whether it was the Governor I worked for or Mrs. Bush. I was out every day doing something proactivly to get our messages out. So it makes a lot of sense to me to be proactive about getting my message of the blog out.

I've been studying and gotten lists of dozens of blogs and their particular interests. When I write an item that might be of interest to another blogger,

I'll email them a link. Sometimes they link back, and sometimes they don't. But I've greatly reduced the percentage of my traffic that simply comes from *Google*. I've been very proactive in generating traffic from other sources and getting quoted around the place. So that's been very satisfying as well.

You mentioned earlier that one of your goals is to be unpredictable. Do you have any other goals for the site?

Sure. First of all, if readers aren't interested by the first paragraph, whatever you say in the second and third paragraphs is irrelevant, because they're going to leave. I've been pleased to see that the time spent on my blog has gone up by about 60–70%, meaning that people are sticking around to read more, to comment more. That's very satisfying.

So, aside from being unpredictable, I'm trying to enhance the initial attraction to get them in the door. I do that with headlines like "Hillary Clinton Shot a Duck Once" or "Obama Team Probe of Obama Team Finds No Obama Team in Propriety." Headlines like that get them in the door. Then, once they're there, I'd like for readers to get a feel for what politics is really like on the inside and how it works.

I want readers to understand why these people that we watch up on the public stage are doing the things that they're doing. When Obama went to Denver to sign the economic stimulus package, a lot of the media were grumbling in Washington, because he could just as easily have signed it there. I wrote a long blog post about what the great attraction is of going to Denver to do it, why they did it that way, the thinking, the strategy, behind it. A lot of people apparently liked that.

I did one item on how a campaign staffer worked the July 4 parade with a candidate, the kinds of things that are happening behind the scenes to enable the candidate to do what he does walking down the parade route.

I've done a lot of those things. When Hillary Clinton got caught planting questions at a public forum, I wrote about how everybody does it, never mind what they say. They all do it, and here's why. But they do it better than Hillary's staff did, and here's how they do it better. That way, I hope, regular people get a feel for it, one, and, two, I hope they go away with at least one or two little things that they learned about politics and how it works.

I also try to throw in a bit of humor. I try to have fun with it and, as I mentioned earlier, because I've written books and am comfortable with my voice, I'm comfortable with letting people see what the fun is.

But I learned, when I was writing the column for *The New York Times*, that it's very appealing if I don't know exactly where the column is going to end because, then, the reader doesn't know either. This is what I call my lingerie theory of communication. It's what you can't see that interests you, that appeals to you. Night gowns, for instance, suggest that there's more there, so you're drawn in. A Japanese garden is the same way. If there's a tree, there's got to be a bush in front of it. If there's a rock, it's got to be partially buried, so that you can't see all of it. The subtle result is that you're drawn in to wonder what it is, to continue to look and see more. So, as I write these items, it's an exploratory trip for me and usually not until about two-thirds of the way through that I realize how it's going to end.

The reaction seems to indicate that, at least with some people, that works, because they're curious about where this idea is going. It's not like your traditional, inverted pyramid news story.

Where do you get your inspiration from?

Blogging is a hand-to-mouth world, and it's a very hungry beast. I find that, when I start to wander around, after two or three places I'll usually find something, and then I'll get busy with that. Because I've got something up pretty soon, I don't end up going to 24 different places.

I do have lots of things sent to me, and I've gone out and arranged for material to be sent to me. And, over the course of the last three years, I've made contacts in various places that follow politics. It's like having a team of scouts out there.

Not everybody sends me something every day but, over the course of a week or two, everybody will volunteer something to me. Some of it I can use, and some of it I can't. I always explain to them why.

I've also created a lot of *Google* alerts for various topics and terms, so that stuff comes to me automatically, including from places that I wouldn't think to go looking.

Who do you have in mind when you blog?

I'd say better educated people who pay attention to current events and who want to learn something. Many of my readers, though, are partisans. What I hope to do is to engage them, either in the sense that they'll be angry with me, or that they'll say to themselves, "Oh yeah, this guy gets it. Finally, somebody's pointing some of these things out."

I love to point things out that have been overlooked. There was a very controversial item a couple of years ago when Michelle Obama was working in a food kitchen. The entire online world wrote about it, and there were lots of pictures at the homeless shelter. And there were lots of pictures of a homeless man taking a picture of her with his cell phone.

I did an item about her doing that, how nice it was, and how First Ladies traditionally do things like that. And, by the way, if this guy doesn't have enough money to buy food how could he afford a cell phone? And, if he's homeless, where would they send his cell phone bill?

Just asking that question ignited the left to pick it up as proof that everybody hates Michelle Obama. The right picked it up as a phony photo-op for Michelle Obama. They can all have their own interpretations, as long as they click on my blog to read about it.

Aside from what you've mentioned already, do you do anything else to attract and retain readers?

Yes, I work very hard on the headline. Take, for instance, the Hillary Clinton story I mentioned earlier. In the fall of 2007, when she was campaigning in Wisconsin, everybody in the online world was writing about how she was going after the NRA vote and the hunter's vote in the Midwest.

I asked myself, "How can we make our item stick out from all the other ones?" The one I wrote was called "Hillary Clinton Shot a Duck Once." If I saw that amidst 50 headlines that said Hillary Clinton goes after the NRA vote, I'd click on that.

When she lost the primary election, I did a news analysis late that night with the headline, "What the Hill Happened?" I try to make the headlines saucy, almost outrageous, and sort of tabloid-like, in a sense, but not necessarily about sex. They're often, I hope, sarcastic or funny like one that I did, "McCain Comes Out Against Deadly Nuclear Weapons, Obama Does Too." I try to have an underlying tongue in cheek quality to it that would make a general reader interested.

I do have a lot of readers from government offices, a lot of the major politicians and, of course, all the television networks. But the person I'm thinking of when I write is a general interest reader who's interested in learning. I'm not necessarily writing for professional politicians. Usually they would know what I'm writing about, but they would also want to know what this guy's telling the world about us.

So I do make some assumptions on the blog. I've had a number of readers tell me that they like the way I assume intelligence on the part of the reader. So, for instance, I never write, "Hillary Rodham Clinton." It's always "Hillary Clinton." I never say, "Senator John McCain (R–Arizona.)" I never do any of that. If it's important that the guy is Republican, I'll just say that he's a Republican. I don't get caught up in this bureaucracy, and I don't want people to think that here comes the name and next to it comes the letters.

I don't go back in time. If it's really relevant, I'll talk about it and put in a link to a previous *Top of the Ticket* post. Then, if people want to know the background of this or that, they can click on it.

When people guest-blog for me, I tell them to take their newsroom girdle off and that we're not in a newsroom when we write this. We're in a sidewalk café talking with a well-informed good friend. So sell it that way, with hand motions and all.

What, in your opinion, makes for a high-quality political blog?

The number one thing is that it needs to be engaging. Number two is that it needs to be informative. I'm not writing this blog to confirm anybody's beliefs which is what many blogs, probably a majority of them, do. You go to this or that blog to be told what you already like, and you might feel better about it for the day. I'm not in that business.

I'm in the business of telling you how this business, and it's a business, works. How silly humans are in this business. How silly they can be. And to process it through my own mind in an interesting way, so that people will want to come back and say, "Well, what do they have up there now?"

So I'd say engaging, informative, and timely, although I've written about things either before or after an event that can stand by themselves because, hopefully, they're elucidating some aspects of it. Unlike a newspaper, it doesn't get thrown away and our blog items live forever.

The stories on the site have a shelf life, but the blog items go on forever. People are still linking to items that I put up last June, still commenting on them. It's satisfying that what you've written seems to have an enduring interest.

**What advice would you give someone who wants
to launch a political blog himself?**

I'd say that your blog needs to do something that other people's blogs don't do. I'd say that there needs to be a reason for me to come to you as opposed to any of the 30 million of us out there. There needs to be a reason for us to come to *you*.

Either you need to say it in a certain way, or you need to teach me things. You have to find that niche and be very realistic. A lot of people think that, say, television journalists just get in front of the camera and talk. I've done enough of that stuff on camera to know that that's not the case.

It's the same thing with blogging. I find that most of my print colleagues, while they're supportive and congratulatory about the blog's success, they don't get it. I think that there aren't that many people from the older print generation who can make the leap into the online world, because it requires a whole different attitude.

When you're in print, you write a good story and it goes on the front page. Six months later the circulation figures come out, and they're either up or down. Who knows whether you had anything to do with it? So you write your story, you leave your phone number with the desk, and you go home. They'll call you with some questions, they fool around with it, probably mess up your favorite part, and it's in the paper in the morning.

When you write a blog, you first have to find something to write about. Then you've got to find an original way to write about it. Then you've got to start promoting it, trying to figure out how you can get it out to the world for people to come across. Especially that last part about promoting it rubs traditional print people the wrong way.

I'd a print editor say to me last October, "You mean to say to me that you'd actually write a blog item that you knew would attract thousands of readers?" I answered, "You bet your sweet ass I would."

He shook his head because you don't do that in the print world. You write a story if it merits writing, and then you put it out there. Somehow the world will find it. So I said to him, "Well, I'm going to have about five million readers this month. How's the print circulation going?" There was dead silence.

They don't get it and, if by now they don't get it, I don't think they want to get it. So I just go about doing my thing. I've never had so much fun in journalism as I've had doing this blog. It's liberating. It's satisfying. It's rewarding. I just can't imagine having a better job.

It's draining and exhausting, and I'm sure ready for the weekend. But, even on the weekend, you'll find me checking my BlackBerry and saying, "Well, maybe I should go put something up on Saturday afternoon."

You mentioned that traditional print journalists just don't get what political blogging is all about. Could you elaborate on that?

Sure. During the monopoly period, newspapers were like pharmacy counters. Every day people lined up at the pharmacy counter to get their daily dose of news. The newspapers handed out the dose of news that we'd decided during the night that people should get. The walked away with it and were fine with that.

But now they can get their own, personally-drafted dose of news medicine from countless sources, so they need a reason to come up to our counter.

I think a lot of the newspapers are still staying behind the counter and say, "Geez, did you notice that there aren't as many people coming up to the counter?" We've got to get out in the parking lot before they go to Wal-Mart and get them into our store.

So I'll go out and actively seek friends online, fellow bloggers that I'll link to. Some of the readers come over here, discover us, and some of them will come back. If they return, I'll link back to that person when they have something of interest to our readers. It works back and forth. I love the collegiality of it.

Are there certain mistakes that less experienced political bloggers should be especially aware of?

Yes, to be boring. You've got to make people want to read it. It's a choice, after all. It's like that old story about the Hollywood mogul who made all these successful movies in the 1930s and then had a bust. He said, "If they don't want to come, you can't stop them."

It's true. You have to make people want to come. They're not going to habitually come over to your place, if they're going to get bored three times a day. Just as they're not going to buy a newspaper or a magazine that tells them things they already know or says it in a boring way.

So it's very competitive. I happen to enjoy that. But I think that a lot of print people got very comfortable in the monopoly years with being oracles. Now they're talking to a dwindling bunch of people on the mountain side, and it's frightening to them.

In the late 1990s, I realized that I'd raised four children, I'd housed, fed, educated, transported, played with, and recreated with each one of them completely on the earnings of newspapers. And not one of my four children read a newspaper. That told me something had mentally changed.

As much as I might, I didn't like the comfort of the old days on newspapers. But even if I had, you can't go back there. You've got to find a new way to do it and, at my age I guess, I'm unusual for finding that. But, as I said, I've never had so much fun. I've never been so excited about getting to work every day, and I guess it shows.

What trends do you see with respect to political blogging?

I'd say that the most prominent trend is the emergence of aggregator type blogs that pull things together for you. That's the appeal of *Google Reader*, for instance. You can have sent to you whatever you want sent to you, and it pulls it together for you every day.

In the future, I think, the majority of people will probably want one, two, or maybe three such places. And those places would have already pulled together the links to the places that this person likes. Just look at Matt Drudge's site, the *Drudge Report*. He has all the links to all the columnists on all the sides. So there's a reason why he gets 20 million hits a day. Even if you don't like Matt Drudge, you go there because you don't have to bookmark other sites.

So I think there'll be more of that, but also more original reporting. And, hopefully, for the sake of democracy, we'll have enough news gathering organizations from which the rest of the blogging world can feed.

If you drive to work in Los Angeles, and I assume it's the same in other places, you're going to hopscotch around from radio station to radio station. But 98% of what you hear was in the *Los Angeles Times* that morning. That's where they get their talking points. And if you look at the front page of the *Los Angeles Times*, you pretty much know what's going to be on the 6pm news tonight. So we do need to have major news organizations with the ability to invest in original news gathering.

6
Nick Gillespie

Like political discourse in the U.S. more generally, the political blogosphere is dominated by liberal and conservative voices. Nevertheless, there are many libertarian sites, of which *Reason Magazine*'s official staff blog, *Hit & Run*, is the most widely read and influential one.

Hit & Run was launched in late 2001 by Nick Gillespie, *Reason Magazine*'s Editor-in-Chief at the time, and Tim Cavanaugh with whom Gillespie had previously collaborated on the satirical web site *Suck.com*. The blog's name, *Hit & Run*, was taken from what had been a weekly news round-up on that site.

Gillespie, who has a Ph.D. in English Literature, currently serves as Editor-in-Chief of *Reason.com* and *Reason.tv*. Aside from overseeing and contributing to *Hit & Run*, he blogs for other prominent political blogs like the liberal *Huffington Post* and the conservative *Big Government*, writes for mainstream publications like the *Los Angeles Times*, the *New York Post*, *The New York Times*, *The Wall Street Journal*, and *The Washington Post*, and is a frequent commentator on the major television and radio networks, including *CNBC*, *CNN*, *Fox News*, *MSNBC*, and *NPR*. The well-known news web site, *The Daily Beast*, has named him one of "The Right's Top 25 Journalists," and *Hit & Run* has been called one of the best political blogs by *Playboy* and the *Washingtonian*, among other publications.

Consistent with *Reason Magazine*'s libertarian philosophy, Gillespie manages *Hit & Run* with very little editorial oversight. The (about) one dozen magazine staff members who contribute to the site are given free reigns, and there's no prior discussion of which topics to cover or subsequent editing of postings. He likens the site to an eighteenth- or nineteenth-century coffee house where, instead of having leaders and followers, the conversation approximates one among equals and runs in multiple directions simultaneously instead of in one predetermined direction. Thus, while the magazine's staff members write the initial postings, these are meant as conversation starters to which the site's ever-growing community of commenters is encouraged to contribute rather than as the final arbiters on given topics.

#####

How did *Hit & Run* come about?

Reason Magazine has been around since 1968. We launched our website in 1994 which, for this type of magazine, was pretty early. I became the Editor-in-Chief of the magazine and the website in 2000. And that's really when we started to focus more on online content and putting everything up for free, trying to come up with original, daily content rather than to roll out the stuff that was in the print magazine.

Then, in 2001, after hemming and hawing for a while, the publisher of the magazine at the time lobbied really hard for us to start a group blog. And, if I remember correctly, *Hit & Run* went live in December of 2001.

We were heavily encouraged by Glenn Reynolds of *Instapundit* who'd started his own blog in July of 2001. A former editor of *Reason Magazine* had also started a blog in 2001. So those were the kinds of examples that helped spur us along.

Our contributors are essentially the magazine's staff and a couple of contributing editors who've had a long affiliation with us. We've around a dozen contributors.

Have you overseen *Hit & Run* since its inception?

Yes. I've been the Editor, the person who oversees it. But one of the things that distinguish *Hit & Run* from a lot of other political blogs is that, from its very inception, we'd a totally decentralized work force. Very few of us are in the same office, and we don't even live in the same time zone as one another.

So there's actually very little oversight on my part. There's no prepublication, editing or scanning of anything. Stuff just goes up. We very much embrace the idea of valuing the opinions, the insights, and the interests of our contributors. So we just let them go.

Similarly, very early we also made the decision, which I think is consistent with the larger impulse of the Web as well as our particular ideology, that we'd have comments. For other sites, like *Daily Kos*, that's a given. But most magazines either don't have comments, or moderate the comments heavily. We just said, "Let's let it rip and try and create a space for whoever is interested in filling it."

What has been the biggest challenge so far?

The biggest challenge has been to produce more content. We all have to produce more content than we did a decade ago. So the challenge has been to institute a regime whereby blogging one to three times a day has become a non-negotiable activity in every editor's workday.

Is that primarily to increase the frequency of postings?

Yes. One of the things that the blog has allowed us to do is to comment on more things. We're an ideological magazine, a message magazine, so one of the things we're trying to do is to apply our frameworks, our methodology, and our ideology to more rather than less stuff.

The blog has allowed us to comment on stories, to create discourse, to call attention to certain things with less investment of time and energy. Indeed, that's one of the organizing functions, or impetuses, of having the blog in the first place.

It was hard, at first, to get staffers to do this, because everybody is busy. But the comments, the immediacy of response to blog posts, really help energize people to write more, to produce more, because you've a sense of an audience that's very immediate and often times very critical, but also very insightful.

Part of *Reason Magazine*'s whole vision of politics, and the blog has helped us further that vision, is to abolish the top-down system where there are leaders, rulers, or wise men telling people, "OK, go stand over there and do this." We don't want to be like movie directors. The relationship between writer and reader is much more leveled, and the blog totally feeds into that.

On that note, who's your intended audience?

There are several overlapping and complimentary audiences. One is certainly readers of *Reason Online* and, more broadly, *Reason Magazine*, self-described libertarians who're interested in seeing their thoughts, their frameworks, fleshed out and critiqued from within a sharpened focus and supplied with new ideas.

Another is peer journalists. We can have an influence by influencing our peers in journalistic circles. *Reason Magazine*'s big story in this respect is John Stossel from *ABC News*. He was a kind of standard-issue, crusading consumer affairs journalist until some point in the 1980s when he came across *Reason Magazine*. It helped change the way he thought about stuff. Now a very *Reason*-like approach to a lot of news is channeled through John Stossel who reaches six to eight million people a week on *20/20*.

We've also had politicians at both the national and local level get in touch with us and say, "These policy ideas you come up with are exactly what we need to fix these issues or problems."

Do you do anything in particular to attract those audiences?

The main way that we attract readers is through the content. The content is king. It's clear, though, that marketing helps, and we do things like send out emails. We develop and cultivate relationships with other bloggers who're both on our side and against us. We certainly cultivate rivalries as well as alliances with other people.

On a more technical level, one of the things that we do is create searchable topics. We've shifted to a backend architecture that takes advantage of automated search engines by putting key words in the URL for individual blog posts.

So it's all about coming up with interesting concepts, making sure they're easily available to people, are readable in form, and give people options to carry them.

What was the original goal for the site?

At first it was an attempt to help serve our audiences. One goal was to put a kind of *Reason* stamp, *Reason* filter, *Reason* lens on more topics in the news, particularly more pressing news cycle stories because, when you work for a monthly magazine, there's a long lead time.

This means a different type of treatment of topics. Our print magazine remains, even among our peers, one of the last practitioners of true long-form journalism, or what I'd call a deeper, longer-range analysis. It's hugely important. But what the blog allowed us to do was to weigh in very quickly on stories of the day as well as to intercede, and hopefully also make an intervention, in daily discourse where we inject information, analysis, and ideas.

So a huge function of the blog was to serve as a kind of rapid response into the topics of the moment and breaking developments. 9/11 is a good example of that. It's not that you're going to change the course of human events by blogging, but it allows you to engage and discuss and analyze things much more quickly.

The other function of the blog, which I don't think we fully understood when we first launched it, was to serve as a virtual community, a kind of third space that allows people who're interested in being part of the community to come and hang out.

It's definitely like a coffeehouse, an eighteenth- or nineteenth-century coffeehouse, model of a conversation where there are some people who're starting and structuring the conversation. But it's very much a conversation, not necessarily among equals, but where the traditional role of authority and subject have very much broken down or have at least become more leveled.

One of the recurring themes of the magazine during the past decade, if not during its entire run, is that we're witnessing a slow and exorable leaching of power from a few kind of nodes in a network to many nodes. Regardless of whether you're talking about traditional authority figures like politicians, priests, stockbrokers, lawyers, or doctors, they're losing power at the expense of end users in a network who're starting to push back and say, "You know what? I'm pretty smart. I know how to live my life. I know what information I have, and I want to have a conversation rather than listen to a lecture." And that's where *Hit & Run* has really developed into something that was totally unanticipated by us. There are regular commenters, and it has developed an interesting, virtual community.

What's really great about it is that it's multidirectional, so that the information will flow in two, three, even four directions as opposed to in one direction like a standard broadcast.

What role do you see *Hit & Run* playing in the political sphere more generally?

We're not interested in partisan policy at all. It's more about creating a different framework of interpretation. One of the ways that I describe libertarianism with a small "l" is that it's a pre-political affiliation that informs your politics. It's actually a step before affiliating with Democrats or Republicans, liberals or conservatives. So one of the things the blog has allowed us to do is to bring our perspective to bear on a wider range of topics, treating politics as a form of symbolic activity rather than as a simple up or down vote.

The blog also serves as a corrective to pronouncements, whether it's from other journalists, from authorities in government, or corporate people. We're able to respond quickly and add a corrective.

Finally, the blog is a kind of staging ground where our contributors can work out their opinions on a topic and get feedback from other journalists who link to, critique, or extend their analysis, or from commenters who say, "No, this doesn't make sense. You're missing the whole point."

Hit & Run is a play space for thinking and discussing what libertarians would do about a variety of issues. We're not utopians in any sense of the word, but our ideology is about creating endless experimentation and innovation in human affairs, what the French philosopher Michel Foucault would call "technologies of the self." The goal is to create alternatives based on changing desires, needs and wants.

So one of the functions of *Hit & Run* is to give a sense of what the possibilities of libertarianism are. What are the strains of libertarian culture, libertarian thought, and how do you imagine possible alternatives to the status quo regardless of what the topic is? When you knit together this flow of 10, 20, 30, or 40 posts a day, five days a week, what does that add up to? Is that an interesting alternative? Does it spark something in somebody's head when they go do something?

How often do you blog yourself, and where do you get your inspiration from?

On average, I probably blog between three and five pieces a day. They are a mix of quick links to something that might be interesting and longer posts on something I've read.

I typically spend half the time looking in Washington, D.C. and half the time in Oxford, Ohio which is a small town outside of Cincinnati. The first site I generally go to in the morning is the *Cincinnati Enquirer*, just to see what their headlines are.

I go to aggregator sites like *Instapundit*, *Google News*, and *Yahoo! News*. My first reach is for news stories. What are the top news stories of the day, and what are the smaller stories that often get overlooked?

I also go to a number of blogs and other new media sites that I find particularly interesting, because they're bringing something different. One of the sites that I'm most interested in is *Splice Today* by Russ Smith, the founder of the *New York Press* which, along with *The New York Observer* in the 1980s, really revitalized alternative newspapers in New York City. *Slice Today* is a mix of stuff he pulls from other sites as well as original content. It's laid out in a fascinating way that's truly using the capabilities of the Web.

Finally, I get a lot of tips from people, which is also really useful. Some are from people who do it again and again, and some are from people who simply say, "I thought you'd find this interesting. Check this out." So, over the course of the day, I try to do a quick link story, I try to do a comment on a news story, and I also try to do something that I call a synthetic blog piece where I take a couple of stories or events and try to provide more of a thoughtful analysis. It could be 300–500 words.

What, in your opinion, are the defining features of a high-quality political blog?

Regularity of postings. Absolutely. Blogging creates a reader expectation that there's going to be something new and interesting regularly.

Another is an appreciation of the two-way, or multi-dimensional, interactivity of the Web as a medium and of the blog as a genre. As a contributor, I've expertise in certain areas, and I can speak with authority on those areas. In other areas I'll cede the fact that my authority is limited. So your audience needs respect in two ways. One is to give them information that's reliable, useful, and interesting. But the audience also deserves respect in terms of you acknowledging the limits of your understanding. So engagement is key.

One prominent conservative blog has a lot of contributors, an almost endless list of contributors. They bitch and moan among each other, attack one another, and have a bull session. Because you get to see a bunch of heavyweight boxers constantly fighting it out and riffing off of each other, it's almost like a jazz ensemble. We also have intra-contributor squabbles and what not, but we're much more directed towards engagement with our audience. We allow our audience to comment, update the comments, and respond to developments within our comment section.

But I think that a sense of friction, energy, and community is absolutely key to any successful blog where you're creating, either between the writers and the readers, or among both, some sense that we're all in the same room. You need to cultivate a sense that this is a space you can go to, to both learn something new and different and be challenged, but also to be accepted and feel a fraternal sense of dialog, or multi-log.

Do you do anything in particular to ensure that *Hit & Run* stands apart in the political blogosphere?

We do a number of things. One is to send a daily email with links to *Hit & Run* postings to pertinent websites. Regardless of whether we're attacking somebody, championing somebody, or simply writing about somebody, we try to make sure that people who're interested are aware of it.

Another thing, which isn't always the case among bloggers, is that we've got an ethic of inclusion, which means that we try to make the conversation as broad as possible. By broadening the conversation, by broadening the basis and the sources of conversation, everybody wins. It's not a zero-sum game. In fact, you grow the conversation. We grow the universe of readers and enhance our ability to at least get people to think about things in a different light.

Why do think *Hit & Run* has been so successful?

I think it's partly due to the talent of the individual contributors, skimming and bringing the stories or ideas or concepts that wouldn't otherwise be voiced. A lot of it has to with the individual contributors and the fact that they've interesting filters and draw an audience.

Another reason is our ideological framework of libertarianism with a small "l." It's of great interest to many people and it fits exceptionally well with the increasing shift from centralization to decentralization, in economic power, in telecommunications, and in life style. I think the general vibe and the general mentality of *Hit & Run, Reason Magazine* and, more broadly, of libertarianism with a small "l" comports very well with that.

So we've finally been given a space. It's kind of like the student center where we for decades have been denied a meeting room. We now have a meeting room. And the great thing about the Internet is that it's infinite. You can seat as many people as your server can withstand, which is pretty vast.

What advice would you give someone who wants to launch a political blog himself?

First of all, I'd tell the person to write all the time and write in an informed way. Actually, start publishing immediately. And practice in real time and over time. I think affiliating with other people is totally important. It's funny that libertarians often get pegged as rugged individuals going it alone, because it's all about community, imagined community, affiliated community, ideological community.

I'd also recommend the person to do cross-platform blogging, whether it's on *The Huffington Post*, *Daily Kos*, or various right-wing places that also allow for participatory blogging. You need to have your own blog as well as bring your stuff to the attention of other people that you read regularly.

It's important to understand that it's always about being in circulation, refining yourself through associations as well as through a kind of permanent feedback loop. Continuous improvement through interaction. It's important to have as many contact points as possible with the audiences, with the communities that you want to be part of.

I'm a big fan of the factory model, of what you can do to insert yourself in somebody else's assembly line as well as creating and conceiving of your own. That's a powerful model, and it's also one that fits very well with the technology available.

Are there certain mistakes that less experienced political bloggers are especially prone to make?

Yes, and it's true of all kinds of writers, including novelists. There's this presumption that the world was born when you were born, a lack of interest in the past and what has already been done. I find that off-putting.

And then there's this uneven split between a public voice and a private voice, so that it becomes unclear what the purpose of the blog is. It's a mistake to go back and forth between a personal, revelatory motif and a more incisive, public motif. It's not that one is good and one is bad. But mixing the two is amateurish.

How, in your opinion, has the political blogosphere evolved over time?

I think that, in a broad sense, blogs have migrated from being primarily individual efforts to become more sponsored entities. For instance, whereas earlier people working at magazines had a blog on the side, now that blog is sponsored by a specific magazine.

It's high camp and it might have a wide audience. But it's ultimately extremely uninteresting. By the same token, I think that a kind of normalization of blogging in terms of what's expected, what the rules are, has taken place.

There's no question that, as a supplement to mainstream political, ideological, and social discourse, it's all good. For me, the most amazing thing about cyberspace is simply the number of extra words it has injected into everybody's lives. But I do think that there were moments when the political blog was an attempt to escape from a particular set of conventions that restricted people, confined people, both in terms of who could participate and how they could participate.

Ten years into the blogging phenomenon new conventions have formed. While blogging remains an extremely vital, viable, and interesting thing, part of me is looking forward to the next development, which we can't fully anticipate.

Blogging is reaching a level of maturity which is good. The political blogosphere is still very open to new participants, and you can go from zero to hero in a few months, which I think is great and really inspiring. But I'm also looking forward to what comes after blogging. I'm looking forward to the next thing that's going to be participatory, that's going to be revelatory, and is going to deliver some new kind of information, some new kind of conversation that's important.

7
Thomas Lifson

Thomas Lifson, the co-founder, Publisher and Editor-in-Chief of *American Thinker*, a prominent conservative group blog, had little journalistic training or experience in the U.S. when he started his publication, though he'd worked as an editor and columnist in Japan, at *Asahi Weekly* and *NHK*. A self-described "recovering academic," Lifson was a former faculty member at Harvard University where he taught Business, East-Asian Studies, and Sociology and worked as a business consultant for major corporations in Asia, Europe, and the U.S. before he launched *American Thinker* in 2003.

While *American Thinker* is open to all political topics, it's centrally concerned with U.S. politics, foreign affairs, national security, economics, and military strategy. The site is divided into two sections: longer, analytical pieces, written by people who've expertise in specific areas, and a breaking news-style blog to which anyone can contribute.

Lifson's goal for the site is to bring well-informed and intelligent analysis and discussion of various political topics to the broader public. His emphasis on the broader public rather than political elites stems from his respect for people who've not enjoyed the same educational opportunities as he but who, nevertheless, are constantly striving to better understand the world in which they live.

To ensure that *American Thinker* is indeed of value to the broader public, as well as to help cultivate new blogging talent, Lifson spends much of this time teaching the other contributors how to become better bloggers. Much like Arianna Huffington, who launched *The Huffington Post* because she felt that some of the most important voices of our time weren't online, Lifson founded *American Thinker* because he felt that there was a vast pool of talent that wasn't part of the existing intellectual or journalistic elites, and that this pool was waiting to be tapped.

#####

When did *American Thinker* begin publication?

American Thinker began publication in November of 2003 but became a daily publication in January of 2004.

I'd been active on political sites on the Internet before Windows, going back to the DOS era with pay sites like *Town Hall,* which was very different from the *Town Hall* that exists today. It was sponsored by the Heritage Foundation and *National Review.* So I'd been writing essays and contributing to threads for well over ten years by the time we started *American Thinker.*

Additionally, I'd been carrying on a very extensive email discussion of politics with people who subscribed to an email discussion list organized by Richard Baehr, one of our co-founders. Richard wrote observations of politics, and others, including another of our co-founders, Ed Lasky, would write responses. Richard still maintains this email list with hundreds of people on it.

It occurred to me that this was like a subscription-only blog. I thought about it for some time, but it took me over a year to develop the concept for *American Thinker.* The goal was to bring well-informed and intelligent analysis and discussion of public events to a broader public. I didn't want it to become just another group blog.

If there was anything out there that served as a model for us, it would have been *Power Line,* because those are some very smart guys, and there are three of them. There were three of us to begin with who were capable of publishing a couple of very interesting and significant analyses a day.

But, I thought, it'd probably be better to go beyond that and open it up to discovering and developing new writing talent. I hoped that we'd get people with professional and personalized knowledge in particular areas, with lawyers writing about law, physicists writing about nuclear issues, etc.

My sense was that there was a vast pool of talent that wasn't part of the existing intellectual or journalistic elites, and that this pool was waiting to be tapped. So I thought very long and hard about how to structure a site that would allow existing talent, like Richard, Ed and I, to publish but would reach out to others as well.

I aspired to create something like *National Review Online* or *American Spectator,* publishing substantive articles as well as blogs.

What has been the biggest challenge so far?

The biggest challenge, and I really should have anticipated this but didn't think it through carefully enough, has simply been the amount of email. Now, after all these years, we get hundreds of emails a day. You have to sort through those to find the ones that have something of value to say.

Some people have good insights but don't know how to write. Other people know how to write but need to be pushed to get a little more depth, so there's a lot of editing involved when you're developing new talent.

It's not a burden in the sense that this is the mission, and I enjoy it. But my big frustration is that I just haven't had the time to write as much myself as I'd like to.

It's been the biggest challenge as we've grown. I'm very happy and proud about the growth that we've had, and I want to continue growing, of course. But I also want to develop more editorial talent.

Aside from cultivating new talent, what are your goals for the site?

Aside from developing new voices, people outside the conventional elite circles, and host a deeper level of analysis and discussion, I want it to be grounded in a more realistic understanding of human nature.

I'm politically conservative. I don't think there's always a conservative position on an issue, but my view of the political spectrum in the U.S. is that a good part of the difference between left and right is a matter of assumptions about human nature, whether human beings are inherently perfectible or inherently flawed.

I tend to believe that humans are inherently flawed. The founders of the American Republic understood that human beings will take care of their own particular interests, so you have to compensate for that in terms of institutions that balance out all the various interests.

I look for grounding in what I believe is a true understanding of human nature, which is that the project of building a perfect new man, a big project of the left, is hopeless and ultimately counter-productive.

I'm a small government person. And, in foreign policy, I believe the U.S. has a role to play as the shining city on the hill in a classic sense. I believe in the right of Israel to exist, positions like that.

That said, we publish a lot of good, reasonable argument on the site that's contrary to what I believe. I don't necessarily endorse every article that we publish, as we're looking to have an interesting site that'll generate thought and discussion.

It sounds like the primary goal is to serve as an idea generator?

Yes, that was the original and primary goal, to generate new and useful ideas. Now that we've grown to have a very lively comment section, I'm beginning to see that we're a bit of a political community as well.

That's the direction I'd like to take the site for the next few years. I'd like to make it a space for like-minded people to connect with one another, electronically as well as face-to-face. But, honestly, I'm in my mid 60s and social networking software doesn't come naturally to me. Technologically, we're a follower rather than a leader and, until somebody younger takes over, it's probably going to remain that way.

You mentioned earlier that you don't have so much time to blog yourself. But when you do find the time to blog, how do you decide what to blog about?

I blog about what interests me, of course — what animates me. Generally speaking, when I blog these days, it has to be something I care about passionately, because I've to put aside other things to do it.

In the ordinary course of affairs the to-do-list of tasks takes precedence. So it'd be the topics that I know and care about. My own background is quite diverse, as I was educated and taught in three different academic fields. I call myself a recovering academic.

I don't write about Japan that much, although that's one of my fields. I write a little bit about China, although I'm less of an expert on China than Japan. I write about business whenever I get a chance because that's the topic that animates me the most.

Who're you trying to reach with *American Thinker*? Educated people? Journalists? Policy-makers?

I'd say all of the above. But I'd have to take issue with the notion of "educated" people, because I'm probably one of the most over-educated people you could run into. I learned fairly early on in my academic career that William Buckley wasn't kidding when he said that he'd rather be governed by the first 1,000 names in the Boston telephone directory than by the faculty at Harvard University.

By that I mean that people who haven't graduated from college, or even high school, have learned from life in a way that people who've been more cloistered haven't.

So I think of our audience as strivers, people who strive to better understand the world in which they live. And I particularly prize those readers who may not have had the educational opportunities that I or others had, but who're constantly asking questions, thinking, and learning.

Those are the people that I think are the heart of our community, whatever their level of education. They can be college faculty, or they can be people working in blue collar jobs that think, have active minds, and aren't afraid of the truth but rather seek it out.

How about journalists and policy-makers?
Are they also a part of your audience?

I know through various means that we're widely read at those levels and absolutely want to reach them, but that isn't our sole objective. I've always been content driven. I believe that, if we provide the right content, we'll find the recognition.

What, in your opinion, are the defining features
of a high-quality political blog?

The first thing is simply the level of intelligence of the bloggers. I admire *National Review Online* and *Power Line* a great deal. There are also a number of solo bloggers out there who are just terrific, like Jim Hoft at *Gateway Pundit* and Dan Riehl at *Riehl World View*. I love all these more individual blogs. They've a lot of personality as well as iconoclastic thinking.

I'd also say civility, although that's not an absolute value. You can be very amusing but not necessarily civil all the time.

In the end, it really comes down to telling the truth as the person sees it. It's about not omitting the facts that are inconvenient to the analysis.

What do you do to ensure that *American Thinker*
stands apart in the political blogosphere?

I try not to be completely predictable. That's one thing. I like to throw in an article about a topic that nobody would ever think of publishing a piece about. And I love to discover new talent and often spend ridiculous amounts of time with new bloggers. A lot of it has to do with psychology as much as it has to do with the actual writing. So we try to keep the site open to surprises, things that are new and different.

One the other hand, we also try to be reliable. People should know, for instance, that they can come to us for an expert analysis on the Middle East. We've done some tremendous analysis on the Middle East.

So it's a mix of dependability, on the one hand, and room for surprise, playfulness, and humor, on the other.

On that note, one of the biggest frustrations has been that a lot of people think they can write satire. Satire is a difficult thing. I probably have a higher rejection rate for satirical pieces than for any other category. It's well over 90 percent. But I do like to have humor and have added more visual content in the last few years.

**If you were to sum it up, why do you think
American Thinker has been so successful?**

I don't want to sound like a broken record, but I think it's because we're offering intelligent commentary presented with a certain amount of style. We've some very good bloggers. And, as I mentioned earlier, we're offering both dependability and unpredictability.

**What advice do you have for people who want to give
political blogging a try themselves?**

I don't have any generic advice. It has to be tailored to the particular person. If the person thinks he or she has a great deal to say on a wide variety of topics and already is an accomplished writer, I'd tell the person to start their own site.

And, in fact, I've encouraged a number of writers that started out with us to start their own sites. That's terrific. I applaud them and help them every way that I can. But, if you're going to start a site, you need to have new material daily.

If they're not willing to make that level of commitment, and if they feel they might need an editor, then I'd urge that person, if they were one of our writers, to stay with us. But, in general, I do encourage people to start their own sites. It's a wonderful discipline. They also get immediate feedback, in the form of readership statistics, and that's very useful in terms of being the master of your own destiny.

The one bit of generic advice I give to all of our bloggers is to put the reader first. Many people write material in order to demonstrate how much they know, or to put forth a point of view they feel strongly about. But they sometimes forget who the reader is, and what the reader needs to know. They get sloppy about using wordy phraseology, not getting to the point, digressing, writing in the first person too much, etc. So the one piece of advice I'd give people is to look at their material through the eyes of the reader who doesn't know you, who doesn't care who you are, and who needs to be given a reason to read the next sentence of your article and continue all the way through.

**What are the biggest mistakes that less experienced
political bloggers tend to make?**

The biggest mistake is the one I just mentioned, namely the failure to put the readers first. Another mistake is relying on sources as factual that may not be factual. It's important to discriminate among sources. An anonymous blogger is not a definitive source.

These are basic things. Anybody that has made it through a year and hasn't become a laughing stock has learned all those lessons. Aside from that, I'm a bit of a stickler for following intellectual property laws. We try not to use other people's visual materials without their permission. We try to keep quotes under 200 words. These are very common mistakes in the blogging world.

How has the political blogosphere changed since you became involved with it?

First of all I think the influence of the political blogosphere has grown enormously. Our friends at *Power Line* provide a very good example with the Rathergate Memos, which was the first real instance of the blogosphere being responsible for a major story in the American media. Since then we've had any number of other instances where blogs have driven a story.

Another basic change, and this is more the case in the conservative part of the political blogosphere, is that a lot of the new angles, the new takes, the new commentary, the new information, the new analysis, on current events, first emerge in the blogosphere. From there it reaches talk radio and *Fox News* because the other media, aside from conservative newspapers like the *Washington Times*, won't publish it.

Only if it's a really compelling story will the rest of the media not ignore it. I'd say the best example of that is President Obama's bow to the Saudi King, which was completely suppressed by the media for days. This was a story that the media were loath to publish, and tried their hardest to suppress, but it had the virtue of having a compelling visual component. And that couldn't be ignored.

I'd say that at least half the public knows that the President of the United States did quite a bow before the Saudi King the first chance he got to see him. That's a defining fact that wouldn't have achieved any notice whatsoever without the bloggers analyzing it.

On the other side of the political spectrum, I think it's fair to say that blogs like *Daily Kos* and *The Huffington Post* have had an enormous impact on the Democratic Party and have strengthened the left. I give them credit for that. That's a huge achievement. Whether it's good for the country is another question that we don't need to discuss.

I also think it's fair to say that much of the initiative for what I call the national discussion now comes from Web publications. And there's a reason for that. In fact, I think the reason is almost more interesting than the phenomenon itself. The reason is that all the traditional media are highly structured bureaucracies with career professionals who've been socialized into a particular way of thinking, and that includes the conservative reporters at *Fox News*.

Those people have been socialized into the norms of journalism, the straight jacket of journalistic thinking, whereas there's really open access in the electronic media. A guy like me sitting in his study in Berkeley, California has created a site that reaches almost every country on earth.

I looked a couple of days ago. The only places we're not read are in a couple of African countries as well as North Korea. We've a six figure daily readership. That's open access. It cost me several thousand dollars to start up *American Thinker*, but that's pittance in the world of journalism.

So with the rise of the blogosphere you've a much broader array of talent, socialized in a much broader array of backgrounds, who're analyzing the data that are now ubiquitous via the Internet. You can find all kinds of things. And you can translate those things that aren't available into English. So we've many more minds with many different backgrounds analyzing data. It would be expected that a broader array of backgrounds analyzing a broader array of information would come up with more insight and would tend to drive the conversation. I believe that's exactly what has happened.

The interesting thing is that, for whatever reason, those voices have gotten more powerful on the left than they have on the right. I think the establishment of the Republican Party doesn't pay as much attention to the conservative Internet media as does the establishment of the Democratic Party. For some reason, the Republicans are more conservative in their approach.

8
Eric Garris

Unlike the other political blogs profiled in this book, *Antiwar.com* is devoted to a single cause: the opposition to all forms of war, military intervention, and the associated loss of civil liberties. Founded in 1995 by Eric Garris and his fellow libertarian, Justin Raimondo, the site was launched in response to the Clinton Administration's military interventions in the Balkans. Subsequently, the site has opposed the Bush Administration's (and now the Obama Administration's) wars in Afghanistan and Iraq, among many other armed conflicts around the world involving the U.S. and other countries. *Antiwar.com*, which is the most widely read site of its kind on the Internet, operates under the auspices of its parent organization, the California based Randolph Bourne Institute, a non-profit, educational institution dedicated to promoting a non-interventionist foreign policy for the U.S.

Garris, who serves as *Antiwar.com*'s Managing Editor and Webmaster, as well as Webmaster of another of the blogs profiled here, Lew Rockwell's *The LRC Blog*, has been a political activist for more than four decades. He was a prominent member of the left-wing Peace and Freedom Party in the early 1970s, after which he left the party and joined the Libertarian Party. In the early 1980, he helped establish, with Raimondo, the Libertarian Republican Organizing Committee, to work as a libertarian caucus within the Republican Party. More recently, as in the case of *Antiwar.com*, Garris has sought to challenge the politics of both the Republican and Democratic parties, arguing that neither of these parties offer effective vehicles for principled libertarian politics.

While Garris' personal politics are libertarian, *Antiwar.com* features contributions from across the political spectrum, ranging from the extreme right (anarchists) to the extreme left (socialists), many of whom file original news reports from within the conflict areas covered by the site. *Antiwar.com*'s reliance on contributions from across the political spectrum is a reflection of the fact that there's a long tradition of anti-war advocacy on both the right and the left.

One measure of *Antiwar.com*'s success in drawing attention to its cause is its six-figure daily readership which includes mainstream journalists, prominent political analysts, and politicians. The site's growing influence has been discussed on television programs such as *PBS*'s "News Hour with Jim Lehrer" and in newspapers like the *Washington Post*.

Garris attributes *Antiwar.com*'s success, in large part, to the efforts to transcend conventional party politics. Instead of adhering to a specific political ideology, or belonging to a particular political party, the site is focused on a single, enduring cause for which it strives to be, in Garris' words, "all-encompassing."

When did you start *Antiwar.com*?

I started it in 1995. But, for the first two or three years, it wasn't much more than a bulletin board where we were posting articles. I was still learning about the Internet at that point.

We really started moving in 1998 after President Clinton started bombing Iraq. That's when we started updating the site in a daily manner and got additional contributors to write for us, as opposed to just posting stuff that we'd gotten from other sources.

During the Kosovo war, our traffic increased fifty-fold. One of the things that differentiated us at that point was that we were able to get reports from Serbia and Kosovo before the major news media outlets or, at least, before they were coming out with them. We broke a number of stories, like the prison bombing by NATO and the bombing of the passenger train.

Both of those stories, along with pictures, appeared on *Antiwar.com* before they were on *CNN* or *NBC*. That was because the Kosovo war was the first war where the civilians in the war were able to get their information out electronically. It was also the first time that bloggers started to really challenge the mainstream news media as far as being able to compete with the information.

It became a full-time occupation for me even before it became a paying occupation. I started working full-time for *Antiwar.com* in 2001 but, by 1999, it already was taking up most of my time.

**You've contributors of various political persuasions.
Has that been a challenge?**

No, it's not really been a challenge. It's given us the ability to be different. We're not left-wing or right-wing; we're anti-war. There's an anti-war tradition that goes back on the left and on the right. Our goal is to bring those traditions together, as well as every other part of society that's against war, or at least against particular ones. The only way we're going to be able to stop wars is by uniting, regardless of our positions on other issues.

Aside from your long-term objective of stopping war, do you have any other, more immediate goals?

Sure. We find that Americans are some of the least informed in terms of news about foreign affairs. And, in these days with instant information, there's really no reason, especially for Americans, to be ignorant of them. When you go to *CNN*, there's very little emphasis on foreign affairs and, even there, it's usually just repetitions of whatever the Pentagon is telling them.

So we're providing an alternative that really is being neglected out there. It's a daunting task, on the one hand, but, on the other, the opportunities are endless.

How are you structured organizationally?

We've a small office in San Francisco. Pretty much everyone else is working in their homes around the country or around the world. So we don't have a centralized location. But we communicate continually via email, phone, and instant messenger. We also have an editorial control system on the computer where the different editors, writers, and other contributors can interact.

What role do you play?

I'm the Webmaster. I pretty much take charge of it every day, even when the Assistant Webmaster is doing things. I'm just totally in love with my work, so it's hard for me to even walk away from it for a day. I also do a lot of the producing of the site myself, even though the individual elements are from all the other participants. We've both paid staff, volunteers, and people who're on stipends, like interns.

Who are you trying to reach?

We want to reach people that are interested in finding out more about foreign affairs. We do want to reach, I don't want to say the elite, but the people who're movers and shakers, and I think that we have. There are a lot of people in think-tanks, in government, who read us and who, I know, support us.

Do you also try to reach journalists?

Absolutely. Especially with the Web, journalism has become a different kind of entity than it was. Before, journalism was very competitive, but it's becoming much more cooperative. So there's a lot more sharing of information. That gives us the ability to reach out and get our points of view across, not just on our own site, but on other sites as well. There are so many tools around now for that. People just have to use them.

Which tools are you thinking of in particular?

The search engines are makers and breakers in terms of your need to get good rankings. You need to get your stuff on there constantly. You need to have enough keywords on the different pages, so that the people who're looking for things can find them. That's a task that somebody needs to do in terms of reviewing what the rules are, how you best attain a higher ranking.

It's unfortunate that so much is dependent on that. But, on the other hand, it's pretty open. If you can work with the system, you can get your information out.

What do you believe is the key to attracting and retaining readers over time?

The most important thing is to have consistent quality, because I've seen sites come and go very quickly. If they start to lose their quality, they'll lose the audience very quickly, and it's hard to get it back. Another thing is the continual reaching out to try and get new readers by getting the postings on other sites, by getting them cited in other sources, and getting them as high a presence on the Web that you can get. That's often a case of just using the technical tools correctly in terms of *Google News*, keyword search, etc.

Aside from consistent quality, what's the hallmark of an outstanding political blog?

I think presentation is important. There are a lot of sites out there, and it's hard to find things when they're not presented well.

I also think it's very important that you've original content combined with a filtered presentation of content from other sources. And then you have to have a focus. That's important. My Assistant Webmaster has a blog for a little neighborhood in Brooklyn. He has about 1,000 viewers a day on this blog, which is not that much. But because it's focused on just that neighborhood, and has cornered the market for information in that neighborhood, he makes $1,500 a month on advertising. Anybody who wants to get information in that neighborhood goes to his blog. There are so many opportunities, and in so many different directions.

On that note, what have you done to distinguish *Antiwar.com* from all the other political blogs out there?

I've done a few things. One thing is that we've a single-word name. It's a shame. There are some good sites out there, but their names are very difficult for people to remember, unless they've heard it many times. *Antiwar.com* is pretty straightforward.

Another thing is that we don't have a single ideology. We don't belong to a single party or focus on the left or the right. We're focused on an issue, and we're all-encompassing within that issue.

A third thing is that we're on the Web constantly. If something happens in the international arena, you can read about it on *Antiwar.com* usually before anywhere else. That's our focus, and that's our focus around the clock, seven days of the week.

Why do you think *Antiwar.com* has been so successful?

I think it's the focus on a very important issue that's probably not going to go away for a long time. And there are a certain number of people out there who realize how important an issue it is to them, and they're the core of the people that have kept us alive both in terms of readership and support. We've a $400,000 a year budget that's paid for entirely by donations that we get from soliciting on our site. That's pretty significant. It's about 4,000 people who give money to us on at least a once-in-a-while basis.

What advice do you have for people who want to launch a political blog themselves?

First, they have to decide why. A lot of people mistakenly believe in the slogan from the baseball movie, *Field of Dreams*: "If you build it, they'll come." I don't want to get anybody in trouble, but I know someone who put $3 million over a year and a half into a site. His traffic is dismal, because he's not really focused on what it is and how he wants to promote it. The problem is that a lot of people think, "If I build it, people will come, because it's on the Web."

You really have to have an idea of what it's going to be, how it's going to be different, and how you're going to get that difference out as a product.

Do you have any other, more specific advice for aspiring political bloggers?

There are successful sites that are all over the spectrum, in every way. It's just a question of saying. "This is what I want. This is why I want to do it." If you want to do a site just because it's cool, you're probably not going to succeed, because you don't have a vision.

You have to have a vision. That's the most important thing. After that you have to make a good product.

Aside from lacking a vision, what are some of the other reasons that less experienced political bloggers fail?

When new bloggers fail, it may be a question of not having enough seasons. They thought they could do it in six months, but it'd have taken 18 months to build it to a point where it'd be self-sustaining.

Another thing is that there's a lot of competition. New bloggers have to break through that, and it doesn't necessarily mean that the best will always break through. But you'd hope that, usually, people are going to want the better quality, especially given the enormous number of choices.

Would you recommend that people venture out on their own, or would you recommend that they get together with one or more like-minded individuals?

I think they probably would do better with a group of like-minded individuals. But every situation is different, and it depends on the person. They might be the kind of person who feels that they could pretty much get it off the ground themselves, and maybe they can. Every situation is going to be different.

Briefly put, how has the political blogosphere changed since you started participating in it?

It's become a much more significant part of the political environment. If you look back, say, five years, political bloggers were laughed off. They were not taken seriously. "Blogger" was almost a pejorative term, whereas, today, it's a powerful term.

I think the political blogosphere is going to continue to expand. And I think it'll be hard for us to even guess what kinds of things we'll see in the next five years. There'll just be tremendous opportunities.

A few years ago, if I wanted to show people a video, I'd have to find somebody who was hosting it and refer them to it. One time, when I wanted to show a video, it cost me $1,000 for the bandwidth. Today, I'd just stick a *YouTube* video right on my site, and it wouldn't cost me a penny. So I think that we've yet to see some of the tremendous things that are going to come just in the next few years. People who're interested in politics are all going to have to get wired. They're going to have to get to the point where they really understand it in order to increase their influence.

9
Tyler Cowen

Tyler Cowen, who together with his fellow economist, Alex Tabarrok, runs one of the world's most prominent economics blogs, *Marginal Revolution*, is known for his wide range of interests. He's the author of more than a dozen academic and popular books on the economics of culture and other topics, writes the "Economic Scene" column for *The New York Times*, and has published a best-selling guide to ethnic dining. Cowen, who holds a named professorship at George Mason University, received his Ph.D. in Economics from Harvard University where his mentor was Nobel Laureate Thomas Schelling.

Consistent with his polymathic reading and writing habits, *Marginal Revolution*, which Cowen launched in 2003, focuses on an eclectic range of economic topics, from the repercussions of the global financial crisis to the latest economics books he's read. As an economist and libertarian, with what he calls a "small l," Cowen's goal is to make the general population more economically literate and, in particular, to shake up and challenge fellow libertarians. His mission isn't to proselytize, but rather to expose people to a mode of thinking that's personal to him. Indeed, one of Cowen's chief complaints about less experienced political bloggers is that they tend to be too partisan, seeking alliances and convincing themselves that only they are right.

Cowen's own, non-dogmatic approach to blogging is evident in his choice of blogging venues. Before he launched *Marginal Revolution*, he blogged for a while for Eugene Volokh's conservative *The Volokh Conspiracy*. Subsequently, he's contributed to several other top political blogs, including the liberal *Huffington Post* and the libertarian *Hit & Run*.

#####

What inspired you to start blogging?

Eugene Volokh asked me to blog. I'd met him at a dinner party, and he had me blogging for his site, *The Volokh Conspiracy*, for a while. That was in 2002. I started up my own site, *Marginal Revolution*, about a year after that. There weren't many very good economics blogs back then, and I already had some experience blogging.

Why did you start out with a co-blogger, Alex Tabarrok, rather than venture out on your own?

A one-person blog can get a little monotonous, and, even though I blog more than Alex does, I think it's nice to have a balance. Alex and I have also co-authored a lot, and we're different enough to be interesting, but similar enough that it'll have a kind of flavor of coherence. I think it has worked well, so I'm very glad I've done it that way.

Did you experience any particular challenges when you first started out?

Sure. Having command of a lot of information, which is the key to blogging, has always been natural to me. But simple things like learning HTML, how to format posts, and getting everything to work has taken me a while.

Aside from that, has the blogging format been a natural fit for you?

Maybe that's for my readers to judge. But it feels natural to me.

Why do you do it?

It's fun. I feel that I've the single best audience in the world. When I think of all the people I know who reads it, it's a way better audience than I ever thought I'd have. So I feel a bit, well, how can I not do it? And I learn a lot. You test out ideas, and it keeps you thinking critically. You have to be open to being wrong, or you'll quickly become an unconvincing blogger.

My personal views tend to be what I'd call "small l" libertarian. But I don't view the blog as a means of proselytizing. Rather, my goal is to shake up libertarians, to take whatever people have and challenge it in some way and get them to think better.

It has also had a lot of beneficial side effects that are great. Maybe that's what keeps me going. But I didn't expect that at the time, things like book contracts, chances to give talks. They were not the original motive.

What was the original motive? Was it to make the general population more literate about economic issues? Or was it to serve as a corrective to how the mainstream news media cover economic issues?

It was more the former than the latter. For me, it's not even mainly about economics. I view the blog as a kind of exercise in a way of thinking that's personal to me. I want to put that forward and expose people to it. And in some broad sense shake them up.

On that note, who're you blogging for?

I guess it's me in a way. I think about what I as a reader would want to see. I've been surprised by how many people out there match up to that. But I don't like to put up posts just because I think more people will want to read them. If anything, I worry about getting too many as opposed to few readers, because that could ruin the comment section.

What do you mean by that?

I think we've one of the best comment sections in the whole political blogosphere. It's really quite good. But there's a scale issue here. It could not survive if we had a million people read us every day. So I'd rather have fewer readers and better comments which I could learn more from. It also makes the blog a bigger draw for other smart readers. So I'd rather have 50,000–100,000 really smart readers than a million less smart readers. And that's where we're at right now.

Do you respond to the comments that you receive?

No, I don't usually respond to the comments. I do, sometimes, if I like some very particular point. If I've made a mistake, I'll admit it. Then I'll respond, but I don't like to debate. There's just not enough time in the day. When I'm traveling somewhere, though, I sometimes meet up with readers, and that's always fun.

What do you do, then, to interact with your readers on a regular basis?

If people write me, I tend to respond to their emails, even if I've nothing to say. I've the sense that, if someone has read you and taken the time to write, you kind of owe them a reply.

But, sometimes, I don't write back. For instance, if I'm asked a question I don't know the answer to or, if I do know the answer, it'd require me to write back a treatise.

How do you decide what to blog about on any given day?

I blog about what I've been reading. So a lot of what I do matches the flow of news. And then there will be purely idiosyncratic things; things that are unique just to me.

Do you aim to have a political impact on the issues that you blog about?

Not really. To the extent that it does, I'm happy. To blog is to have an ongoing dialogue. And part of that is a dialogue with yourself, a dialogue with your readers. That's what drives and organizes it. If the White House called me up and said, "We've changed this because of what you said," I'd be flattered, but don't sit there calculating, "Oh, if President Obama reads it, and I say this, then he'll do that." You'd drive yourself crazy with that sort of thinking.

What needs to be there for you to consider a political blog outstanding?

It needs to be updated regularly and to some extent be self-critical or self-reflective. And the person should read widely on the Web. That's a requirement. There are some very smart bloggers who shall remain nameless. They don't read other blogs or respond to them, and I find what they produce to be a little bit backwards. So it's important to be on the frontier of the debate in the political blogosphere.

What do you mean by "self-critical" or "self-reflective"?

You need to try to develop a sense of your own weaknesses, where you were wrong last time, and what you can do better.

If you blog every day, or even every week, you're going to say a lot of stuff. A lot of it will be either wrong or just not exactly the way you wanted it to be. If you don't admit that to yourself, you're fooling yourself.

There are different ways you can respond to that. One is despair. You can quit blogging. The other is not just to try to be more correct the next time around, but to try to teach your readers how you're learning from your mistakes so they can learn that same skill.

Aside from trying to learn from your own mistakes, what else do you and Alex do to keep the blog as fresh as possible?

We make a point of not planning it too much. We try to keep it genuine and not all gussied up and contrived. The reader should feel we just sat down in our proverbial pajamas, and here's how we think.

What do you mean by a "contrived" approach to blogging?

That would be when people too deliberately follow a news cycle or try to appeal to some audience. It's when people say to themselves, "I know a post on gay marriage gets picked up, so I'm going to write one." In the long run that's all counterproductive. The medium rewards a kind of genuineness. You've got to turn on that flow.

**Put differently, people will figure you out
if you're not being true to yourself?**

Sooner or later, yes. They'll say, "What's the point?"

Why do you think you've been so successful?

I think it's because a lot of blog readers like that philosophy. We've always maintained a tone where people of many different views felt welcome. That's important, and it keeps the comments good.

**What advice do you have for people who want to
launch a political blog themselves?**

You have to post every day or almost every day. And you have to process information at a speed several times the normal average.

If you're not going to do it for real then don't bother. Some people say, "Well, I thought I'd experiment with it and maybe do it once a week." Don't bother, then.

You also need an area you know a lot about. Even if you're blogging about more than that area, you need some field of strength that you can return to and build upon. If you don't have one, it's tough. Take Ezra Klein of *The Washington Post*, for instance. Health care makes up only a quarter of his posts, but it anchors everything he does.

**Are there certain things you wish less experienced
political bloggers would do differently?**

Yes. They're often too partisan and too political. As human beings we're programmed to seek out alliances and tell ourselves, "We're right, and they're wrong." There's some return in that. But I think people way overdo it, and those blogs aren't interesting to me.

Briefly put, how has the political blogosphere evolved since you started participating in it?

It's certainly become more corporate and less about the lone guy in the pajamas. But I wonder if that'll last. It's not clear to me that these mainstream media blogs are worth the money. In fact, I don't see them making money in most cases. So, in the long run, the political blogosphere may become more populated again.

So you can imagine a time when the political blogosphere will, once again, become less institutionalized?

Absolutely. I think the medium will be with us forever. A lot of its roots are in the eighteenth-century pamphlets and diaries of Boswell and Johnson, and that whole English coffee house environment. I don't think it's a fad or a trend at all. I think it's a permanent development that'll reach millions for centuries to come. So being on the ground floor of that is important to me, and to have tried to make it more reasonable rather than just throwing stones.

10
Rogers Cadenhead

One of the great attributes of the political blog as a genre is that it's not static. You can start out with one particular format and, over time, develop that format in an entirely different, yet equally successful, direction. Such has been the case with Rogers Cadenhead's *Drudge Retort*.

The brainchild of Cadenhead, a former journalist at the *Fort Worth* (Texas) *Star-Telegram* and the author of more than 20 books on computer-related topics, and Jonathan Bourne, a comedian and television sitcom writer, *Drudge Retort* began as a very successful liberal parody of Matt Drudge's widely read conservative website, the *Drudge Report*, in 1998. Indeed, the site had and still has virtually the same look as the *Drudge Report*, with the same page layout, typography, and style of headlines. The only noticeable difference is that the *Drudge Retort* has a yellow rather than a white background, implying that Drudge is a "yellow" (or tabloid) journalist.

While the *Drudge Retort* started out as a parody site, written by Cadenhead and Bourne themselves, Cadenhead turned it into a group blog (or "social news site," as he prefers to call it) to which all readers could contribute in 2003. Cadenhead sees the site as a vehicle for readers to share and discuss the news among themselves. He serves as the site's Editor, selecting which of the numerous submissions he receives daily will be featured, with the right-hand column of the front page reserved for those postings that have garnered the most reader attention and discussion. Despite Cadenhead's own liberal politics, the site's open to contributors of all political persuasions, including radical conspiracy theorists of all stripes.

Although the *Drudge Retort* is no longer a parody site, Cadenhead hasn't been able (or willing) to shed his past as a prankster completely. In 2005, he was the subject of much media coverage and discussion in the political blogosphere when he registered the domain name benedictxvi.com several weeks before that name was chosen by Pope Benedict XVI, joking that he'd offer it to the Vatican in return for two nights at the Vatican hotel, a mitre (a bishop's hat), and complete absolution for the third week of March, 1987. When those "demands" weren't being met (the Vatican, not surprisingly, never responded), he donated the domain name to the Internet-based charity *Modest Needs*.

#####

Why did you start the *Drudge Retort*?

I started the *Drudge Retort* in 1998 together with a television writer by the name of Jonathan Bourne. The goal was to satirize the *Drudge Report* with fake news stories, similar to what you see on *The Onion* today. And we did it during the height of the Clinton impeachment crisis.

We did it for about two and a half years and received quite a bit of attention. It seemed like the logical thing to do, especially since both Jonathan and I are politically liberal, and Matt Drudge is politically conservative. We thought we could have some fun with it. After the impeachment was over, it seemed like you almost couldn't compete with the news in terms of being more farcical than some of the thing that were happening.

So we eventually threw up our arms in despair and, even though we weren't updating the site regularly, people kept coming. In the run up to the 2004 presidential election, in 2003, I decided to adopt a community blog format.

We adopted a format where I'd post news stories and users could contribute their own as well, and that took off. We adopted the slogan, "Red meat for yellow dogs," to convey that we were primarily going after a liberal audience.

But the format itself was open, and the audience was diverse, so over time we've gotten an ideological mix of users, including quite a few conservatives. And some people whose politics are harder to define, 9/11 truthers, birthers, every other form of conspiracy known to man. So it's an interesting site.

I've noticed. How has the experience been so far?

It's been a gratifying development. I didn't know back in 2003 that it'd reach such a large audience, that the format would be appealing to so many.

What are your goals for the site?

Although it's aimed at Democrats, I've never been a particularly fire-breathing partisan. So the strongest goal of the site is to share the news and to provide a place for people to discuss the issues. I'm happy with the fact that it's more ideologically diverse than some of the other, major liberal and conservative sites like *Daily Kos* and *Little Green Footballs*.

**Was that also the original goal, or was the original goal
more political in nature?**

I was hoping that John Kerry would win and, at the time, political blogs were still finding their feet. So I was hoping to help create the infrastructure for a strong liberal media machine that would give Democrats a counterpoint to talk radio and cable television which are both still Republican-dominated.

But, over time, it became more about carrying the news and feeding the audience that found the site. It's still focused on Democrats and liberals, but if President Obama does something disastrous, we're not going to avoid the news. If people are talking about it, and it's a political story, I'd rather see them talking about it on the *Drudge Retort*.

**What role do you see the *Drudge Retort* playing
in the political sphere more generally?**

At times it's a corrective to the mainstream media and, at other times, it's a source for finding and recommending strong reporting in the mainstream media. A few years ago there was a great journalist by the name of Anna Badkhen who covered the war in Iraq for the *San Francisco Chronicle*. At the time all the coverage of the war was processed stuff, from the generals, from the politicians, from the pundits.

We weren't seeing anything about what was happening on the ground, but her stories were about what it was like to be a soldier in Iraq. It was great stuff. There's so much information out there that even a good journalist at a large newspaper isn't always going to be noticed. And, as a former journalist myself, I'm happy to help find some of these people who're doing great work.

**How do you decide what to include on the blog? You obviously
receive a huge number of submissions every day.**

We start with the submissions that have been sent in over the last 24 hours. I try to find stuff from that to share. The site is structured in such a way that newer stories cause older stories to scroll off, usually within 24 hours. And the stories that draw the most discussion stay around for an extra 12 hours. Although I don't explain it on the site, the right hand column on the front and back page features the stories that have drawn the most attention.

So I look at the content of the stories as well as how much attention they've drawn from other users to decide what to promote on the front page. I decide what goes on the front page, and users control the back page. So it's a mix. I also use RSS feeds to scan some of the big news sites like *Reuters*, *The New York Times*, and the *BBC*.

Who's your intended audience?

I'm primarily trying to find stories that would be of interest to liberal Democrats. But I take a very expansive view of that definition. We don't really stop, when a news story is happening, and worry about whether Democrats are going to like it more than Republicans, and vice versa.

It's interesting, sometimes, when the reaction to a story is completely against my judgment of its news value. The Kelo Decision came down a couple of years ago, which is where the Supreme Court validated the taking of private property for private commercial use through eminent domain. The users of the *Drudge Retort*, left, right and otherwise, went completely nuts. They were in a rage. They thought it was one of the worst Supreme Court decisions ever. So, subsequently, our site covered the Kelo Decision extensively. Honestly, and unfortunately, I've to admit that had it been solely up to me, it wouldn't have gotten as much play, because I just didn't see it as being as important as did the users.

Aside from creating a sense of community, do you do anything else to cultivate a loyal readership?

It's the main focus, although I probably haven't done a good enough job of rewarding regular readers, noting their contributions as well as I could. I get so much feedback, though, that I'm always mindful of who's there and why they are there.

What, in your opinion, are the most essential features of a high-quality political blog?

I'd say that it quotes sources and allows comments. One thing, though, is that liberals realized faster than conservatives that a community-driven blog is stronger than an individually-authored blog. One of the stereotypes of Democrats is that we believe in grassroots media, while Republicans are more comfortable with top-down efforts. And that is reflected in the blogs. Glenn Reynolds of *Instapundit*, for instance, is personally linking to things with no comments, and it's all generated by him. *Daily Kos*, on the other hand, which even from the early days was accepting user diaries from everyone, is a boisterous and compelling mix of hundreds of people.

So I think that a good political blog accepts information from its users, and preferably in an interactive way, rather than simply chooses from behind the scenes. I read Andrew Sullivan, the conservative blogger. One thing that bothers me, though, is that not only does he not want comments but, when he accepts email, he doesn't name his contributor. The only person who gets any play on his blog by name is himself. I like the fact that, while we're having this conversation, there are a bunch of people using the *Drudge Retort* to share news. People aren't getting told what the news is, they are deciding it for themselves.

On that note, why do you think the Drudge Retort has been so successful?

I think it's been a success because I decided to open the doors to the readers. Had I just written it on my own, which was my original thought back in 2003, I don't think it'd have found such a large audience. They have really taken to the format, which borrows heavily from the one by Matt Drudge.

It's one of the things about the *Drudge Report* that I don't think gets enough credit, although he gets plenty of credit for other things. His plain, pedestrian format hasn't changed since 1996. Professional media dress so much on the front page that you don't know where to go. It's nice to go to the *Drudge Retort* or the *Drudge Report* and see a top-down list of current stories. Other blogs haven't adopted that format.

What advice would you give people who want to launch a political blog themselves?

The first thing I'd tell them is to start blogging immediately and to make their own mistakes. It's kind of against the nature of any Web publishing to do a lot of planning. It's better to launch something and to iteratively learn from the operation of the site than to try to make a bunch of plans about what you think is going to happen.

The *Drudge Retort* was originally a parody site, published by Jonathan and myself, and it's now a social news site with thousands of users, largely because of what I learned while running the site.

It's also much more satisfying to get immediate feedback. Throw something up there and, regardless of whether it's good or bad, you'll learn from it.

Your advice, in other words, is simply to start experimenting?

Exactly. But I do think there are certain things that'll make a site more successful than others. The blog format tends to reward constant updates over "waiting-till-you-have-something-really-good-to-say." The immediacy of the format tends to reward people who write early and often. And community feedback is essential. Other bloggers do things differently, but I think you need a comment box. It can be a real godsend for coming up with interesting content, and for making people keep coming back. The people who keep making you come back to the trough all day long are going to be the most successful.

Have you noticed any mistakes common to less experienced political bloggers?

One thing that political bloggers, especially those who come to blogging from a professional environment, have a hard time doing is to share anything about themselves. Blog readers tend to assign authenticity to people who talk about themselves. It's hard for readers to make a connection if you're just going to stick to the meat of the matter, and you're not going to say anything about yourself.

Also, when I was in journalism school at the University of North Texas, we learned about the partisan journalism of the nineteenth-century where political parties had their own newspapers. That's one of the reasons you still see newspapers called *The Democrat* today. I preferred it to the Walter Lippmann style of detached reporting. I'm really tired of stories saying, "Here's one side, and here's another side," without telling you who's right, because the journalist is afraid of having an opinion.

How, in your opinion, has the political blogosphere evolved over time?

I think the political blogosphere rose from nothing to become a fairly significant site of dialogue in this country. You see it with stories that have been broken, like the Trent Lott story or Rathergate. Blogs can be an effective way to get around the media filters and break stories.

Are there any particular trends that you're not so happy about?

Yes. One of the more dismaying, recent trends is that, since blogs reach such a wide audience, stories they don't get right are still percolating up though the media. A good example of that is the conspiracy theory that former Governor Sarah Palin isn't the mother of her youngest child. I wrote a lot about Sarah Palin when she emerged as the Vice Presidential candidate and never read about that story, because that was a crazy theory. There was no evidence for it.

Yet, because a *Daily Kos* diarist wrote about it, updated the post regularly, and was indexed all over the place, that story didn't need the mainstream media to give it any creditability. It was everywhere, to the point that Sarah Palin finally had to address it herself. Yet, if you look at it, there was nothing there.

There was no evidence of such a farfetched thing happening. And, over time, there was more and more evidence against it happening, yet the blogs went nuts with it. The left-wing bloggers, of which I'm one, went nuts with it. I didn't promote it on the front page, but I didn't exclude it from what users posted on the back page, because I don't do that. It wasn't a shining moment for the blogs.

A good example from the other side of the political spectrum was the crazy story about a McCain staffer from Pittsburgh who carved a "B" into her forehead and claimed it was a hate attack. Right-wing bloggers went nuts with that.

It's a shame when this medium we've created doesn't get something right because it's better to be fast than right. That's a disappointment I hope we can find a way to correct.

11
Lew Rockwell

It's safe to say that, among the political bloggers profiled in this book, none have more radical views than the self-described libertarian anarchist and author of *The LRC Blog*, Lew Rockwell. The avowed goal of his blogging and other political activities is to do everything he can to undermine the state. Rockwell is also highly critical of the mainstream news media, eagerly awaiting the day where news organizations like *The New York Times* go out of business. Thus, Rockwell celebrates the emergence of political blogging which, as he sees it, has helped diminish the importance of the mainstream news media and offered more radical voices like his own the kind of public platforms they were rarely able to obtain before.

Rockwell has had a long and distinguished career as a libertarian organizer and activist. Prior to launching *The LRC Blog* in 1999, he served as Congressman Ron Paul's Chief of Staff, as consultant to Paul's 1988 Libertarian Party campaign for President of the United States, and as Vice-Chair of the exploratory committee for Paul's run for the 1992 Republican nomination for President. In 1982, he founded the Ludwig von Mises Institute, a scholarly organization promoting what's known as the Austrian School of Economics, a branch of economics devoted to radical free-market capitalism. Rockwell served as President of the Institute until 2009 when he became Chairman of the Board.

As someone whose views fall well outside the US political mainstream, and who has little but disdain for the established political parties and the mainstream news media, Rockwell neither seeks to influence politicians or journalists through his blogging. Rather, his intended audience is ordinary citizens and, more specifically, young people as they are far more open to anarchist ideas in his experience.

To attract that audience, and to ensure that readers keep coming back for more, Rockwell strives to always have new, yet ideologically consistent, content and, most importantly, to grab readers' attention by being thought-provoking and offering views they're not going to get elsewhere.

#####

What inspired you to launch *The LRC Blog*?

I was inspired by Matt Drudge's *Drudge Report*, although I don't share many political views in common with him. But I thought his format was very interesting. That's what really got me into it.

You're the head of the Mises Institute. How does your blog fit in with your other work at the institute?

I see it as allied, but entirely separate, because the institute isn't a political organization. In fact, we're non-political. Blogging gives me a personal outlet because I'm interested in so many things. And I can do it far more freely because the Mises Institute is a tax-exempt, scholarly organization. So *The LRC Blog* offers my own views on anything of interest to me.

How has the experience been so far?

It's been thrilling. One of the things that I dislike about the mainstream media is that I see them as versatile state media. It's true that, with the exception of *NPR* and *PBS*, the national media aren't directly state owned, but they're certainly joined at the hip with the state, whether it's *The New York Times*, *The Washington Post*, the *Los Angeles Times*, the *Chicago Tribune*, the television networks, or cable news. Obviously, *MSNBC* is different from *Fox News*. But I see them all as spokesmen for the state or state programs, whether it's the welfare state or the latest war.

I see myself as a dissident so, obviously, I'm thrilled that the Internet has made it possible for people like me, who never could get a hearing in the mainstream media, to get the word out.

I remember the old days where it was a huge deal when I was able to publish an op-ed column in a newspaper. I could spend days writing and editing it, going back and forth with the editor. So the fact that I can immediately say what I want to say without the censorship that operates in the mainstream media is very thrilling.

What goals are you trying to further through your blogging?

I'd like to abolish the state. I'm an anarchist, and I don't believe in the state. So that's my long-term goal. I want to do everything I can to diminish, demean, undermine, and subvert the state apparatus. We live in the United States under the biggest government in the history of the world. It's a far bigger operation than the Roman Empire, the British Empire and the Communist Empire.

Because it's a semi-capitalist system, the state has, of course, far vaster resources than it did in a socialist system and can do far more damage. So I want to do everything I can to oppose that, such as working against a fully socialized medical system. Actually, it's a fascist medical system, a combination of the big pharmaceutical companies, private doctors, private hospitals, and state hospitals, all run by the government.

I think we're living in a time where all the things that I've been most concerned about ever since I was a teenager are coming to fruition in a very alarming and quick fashion, under President Bush and now under President Obama.

It sounds like you see your blog as a subversive mechanism?

Yes. I want to undermine the state, and the state depends on consent, because it always represents a small minority. They can't live the life of Riley off the rest of us if they're not a small minority. It's disguised as democracy, which is one of the greatest inventions of the state in terms of its legitimization.

I want to point out to people what I think is the core libertarian insight that can change everything if one is ready to accept it, namely that the state is as a gang of thieves written large. It operates exactly as a gang of thieves does in the private sector. Or, to paraphrase Lysander Spooner, the great nineteenth-century anarchist, the difference between a highway man and a Congressman is that the highway man doesn't ask you to call him honorable. That's actually the only difference.

We've this vast apparatus of compulsion and coercion that operates by theft, killing, slavery, and conscription. I want to do everything I can to undermine that. I want to do everything I can to undermine the consent and make people try to understand that the use of violence or the threat of violence against the innocent is always illegitimate. That's true whether it's a mugger on the street or the Governor of New York State.

Where do you get your inspiration from when you blog?

I'm influenced by the news cycle. Generally, I'd say that the most useful thing about the news cycle is that it bugs me. I'm outraged by the various things that are going on, so that's an inspiration. Obviously, I gain knowledge, too, but I think one has always to be very careful. There's a smokescreen. The mainstream media are generating a smokescreen, trying to hide a lot of propaganda. The U.S., for instance, is not interested in democracy and independence in Iran. They want to re-establish Iran as a puppet state of the U.S. That's what actually is going on. They're not interested in freedom for anybody.

It's always been true, but it became especially clear during the Bush regime and now under Obama, that democracy and freedom overseas means U.S. control. What bothers them about Cuba, what bothers them about Iran, is not the internal structure of the regimes there, but the fact that they're giving a thumb in the eye to Uncle Sam.

Considering your strong political views, are you trying to reach policy-makers with your blogging?

No, I'm certainly not writing for policy-makers, all of whom I think are bad people and already have their minds made up. I think that's true of journalists, too, for the most part. I try to word it, instead, for young people. That's who I want to recruit. That's where the future lies. I think that young people are far more open to anarchist ideas, to radically different ideas than they'd get in their classroom, the newspaper, or on television.

Obviously, I'm interested in people of all ages, even people as old as me. But young people are the ones I want to attract. Their minds and their hearts are more open to radical ideas. As we get older, human beings tend not to be as open.

What do you do to attract readers to your blog?

I want to build a cadre, and that requires having people come back, if not on a daily basis, then at least frequently. So I always try to have different content, yet to remain ideologically consistent.

What would you say are the defining features of a high-quality political blog?

Good writing and independence of thought. That can include people on the left, in the middle, or on the right. I don't know exactly where to place myself on that spectrum since there's both a left-wing and a right-wing component to being an anarchist.

Do you do anything in particular to make your blog stand apart in the political blogosphere?

I simply try to be interesting to people. I want people to know that, when they come to my site, they're getting a view that they're not getting anywhere else.

Why do you think you've been so successful?

I think it's because my site is extremely interesting and thought provoking. Obviously, one may not agree with everything or even anything. But it'll always be interesting and thought provoking. I think that grabs people, and that's certainly my intention.

What advice would you give people who want to launch a political blog themselves?

I've been asked that question before, and I always tell people that they've got to be interesting. It can't just be "I""I""I." You always have to focus on the reader. Research shows that people make a decision about whether to stay on a site within tenths of a second. So you have to grab them and be interesting. You can't be boring.

You also have to be welcoming to your readers and always reply to them when they write to you. You have to do so politely, even if they're very critical of you. I get a huge amount of email, but I think it's important to reply to people who write to me and acknowledge when I get an idea from somebody. That also brings in all kinds of new material, and that's very important too.

Are there certain things you wish less experienced political bloggers would do differently?

Yes. I've seen blogs where people chronicle (and it's almost like a joke to me) everything they do in their life. People are too self-obsessed. I think that, instead, you have to focus on other people, and what other people are interested in. You also have to focus on the things you want to warn people about or that you think are interesting, but that they're not getting from the mainstream media.

How has the political blogosphere changed since you started participating in it?

It's obviously expanded tremendously and that has had the wonderful effect of undermining the traditional media. I keep waiting for *The New York Times* to go out of business, for instance. In fact, I'm sure it'll happen. In my youth it was like a colossus all over the globe. Now it's shaky. The political blogosphere has helped bring that about, and that's fantastic.

I see that the state and its tentacles are always trying to grab everything in the political blogosphere, like they do everything else. But they can't actually do it. There's absolutely no doubt in my mind that if the state and its affiliated intellectuals had known what would happen with the Internet, they'd have outlawed it. They're very unhappy about it, and that's very good.

The power elite is trying to bring the political blogosphere to its knees, but they haven't been successful, and I think and hope they're not going to be successful. Their traditional media are going down, and I hope that continues. In the meantime, we all just have to scramble and try to keep readers interested and achieve our own larger goals.

12
Jim Hoft

One of the remarkable things about the political blogosphere is the sheer diversity of backgrounds that its practitioners bring to it. Take, for instance, Jim Hoft, the author of the widely read conservative blog *Gateway Pundit*. Before he took up blogging, Hoft worked as a model and actor, participating in numerous television commercials and print ads as well as several television shows and films. In an earlier life (or so it seems), he researched microbes in the Mississippi River, having received a bachelor's degree in Biology from Loras College in Dubuque, Iowa.

Like many other conservative bloggers, Hoft started blogging in the aftermath of the 2004 presidential election. He was inspired to do so by the scandal surrounding former *CBS News* Anchor Dan Rather's use of forged documents about President George W. Bush's service in the Texas Air National Guard. The scandal, which subsequently became known as Rathergate, is one of the most prominent examples of the power of political bloggers to effect changes within the mainstream news media establishment (Dan Rather resigned under duress and four top executives at *CBS News* were fired.)

Hoft is well-known, both within and outside the political blogosphere, for his blogging about various democracy movements around the world, including those in Iran, Iraq, Lebanon, and Kyrgyzstan. He's a prominent member of the St. Louis Tea Party Coalition, appears regularly on television and radio talk shows, and his blogging and other political activities are often cited by other conservative luminaries like Rush Limbaugh and Sean Hannity.

While Hoft took up blogging because of his passion for politics, he's managed to convert that passion into a lucrative career. Since 2010, his blog has been hosted by *Right Network*, a new television network founded by Kelsey Grammar, which pays him for his efforts. But that's the result of all the hard work he puts into it: he spends at least 10 hours a day blogging.

#####

Why did you decide to take up blogging?

I started blogging after the 2004 presidential election. It was a really exciting time, and I was looking for news sources where I could find more information. I'm a conservative, so I found a couple of blogs that were active at that time, like *Power Line* and *Little Green Footballs*.

When the Dan Rather story broke, it was exciting to follow the story and see how blogging worked. People with different kinds of expertise contributed and were able to break open the story. A little later on, Glenn Reynolds' book, *The Army of Davids*, came out, capturing what we were seeing.

So you wanted to be part of that larger blogging movement?

Yes, it really excited me. I started to follow the blogs more closely and, after the election, I decided to start my own blog.

How was the experience when you first started out?

I'm one of the few bloggers who started out with the *Blogger* software from *Google,* and I'm one of the few that has stayed with it. A lot of bloggers start with *Google*'s *Blogger* or *Blogspot* and then move into a different format. But I stayed with *Blogger*. I've been very happy with it and have seen it get better over the years.

As with anything else on the Internet, there are so many more things you can do today that you couldn't do before. When I first started blogging, there was only one blog that had videos. It couldn't stay in business because it cost too much for the bandwidth. It's gone. Today, you don't even think about it. You slap videos on your blog all the time.

What has kept you going all these years?

Let me answer you this way. Here I am, in St. Louis, Missouri, in the middle of the country, and it's just amazing to me that I can sit in my home and break so many stories. I see so many stories that aren't being reported from a conservative side. And that's something I really want to do, to get some of the other news out that isn't being reported in the mainstream news.

So you see yourself as a corrective to the mainstream media?

Oh, definitely.

Do you also try to reach policy-makers with your blogging?

I do. In fact, I've met quite a number of different politicians since I started blogging. During my first two or three years, I concentrated on the democratic movements around the world, like the Feeder Revolution in Lebanon, the Tulip Revolution in Kyrgyzstan, and the Iraqi election. The latter one was very moving to me. I was just amazed by the bravery of those people.

So I did a lot of blogging about various democratic movements and was actually invited to some events at the United Nations. I was also invited to Prague for a democracy convention where President Bush spoke. While I've met a lot of politicians, the people that impressed me the most were the dissidents. They don't enjoy the same freedoms that we enjoy. I was so impressed by their courage and their stories. Most of these people have amazing stories.

How many hours a day do you spend on blogging?

I'm obviously putting more time into it than I did when I first started out. I spend at least 10 hours a day blogging. I started off slow, writing one or two posts a day. In 2005, I started getting attention and started putting up six or seven postings a day. Today, I generally put up 10 to 14 posts a day.

Where do you get inspiration from for all those postings?

Like most bloggers, I have a few websites, my favorites, which I go to every day to get some good stories. They include: *Free Republic*, *Hot Air*, *Instapundit*, *Little Green Footballs*, and *Michelle Malkin*.

Aside from these major, conservative blogs,
where else do you go on a regular basis?

As I mentioned earlier, I've been interested in various democratic movements around the world. There have been several stories from Iran that I've reported on. So I follow some Iranian websites, and I've a couple of Iranian friends who're feeding me stories.

I've broken different stories that weren't positive towards the regime. They've actually written about me on the official Parliament website. To me, that was amazing. They weren't threatening me but called me a war monger. They weren't happy with what I was doing.

Who do you have in mind when you blog?

I'm a conservative, so I expect to have a conservative audience. It always feels good to know that I'm read by people who I respect, like recently when I met David Limbaugh, Rush Limbaugh's brother, who's an author himself. I also understand, though, that with greater readership, I'm going to get some people on the left who just want to catch me make a mistake or something. So I've readers like that, too.

What do you do to retain readers?

It's always helpful to develop personal relationships with your readers, so when I get really good comments, I'll move them up to the post itself.

I get a lot of emails, and I try to respond to a lot of them. I think that helps, too. When you promote your work, it's important not to spam 100 people. It impresses me when I know that what somebody wrote was just for me. If the email is just for me, I'd certainly give it more attention than if I noticed somebody spammed 100 people with something they wrote.

On that note, what makes for a high-quality political blog in your opinion?

It'd definitely need to be continually updated throughout the day, although that's not as important on the weekend. Most blogs, including some of the bigger ones, don't put up as many posts on the weekend.

But if you want to be taken seriously, you have to have continually new material. That's the biggest thing. If you want to build your readership, you also have to share your information and reach out to other bloggers and promote your work. There are some excellent bloggers out there with terrific skills who people don't know about because they're not reaching out to other blogs.

What do you do to stand apart from all the other political blogs out there?

I'm consistently putting out more material, new material. I'm also consistently sharing that material. You'd be surprised how many people don't do that. You just won't be taken seriously if you don't do it.

I'm also able to find stories that are interesting, and that other people find interesting. My readership has doubled in the past year, so I'm obviously finding the right stories.

Why do you think you've been so successful?

I think it's because I've been doing this for a long time and have been very consistent with it. So many bloggers out there just quit. There are millions of people who put up a couple of posts and never come back to it. And, as I said earlier, I'm able to find interesting stories and communicate them in an interesting, entertaining way.

**What advice do you have for people who want to
give political blogging a try themselves?**

People ask me for advice all the time. And it just has to be the same message. You have to be willing to put in the hours, and you have to be willing to reach out. And you have to be respectful when you reach out.

**Do you find that many bloggers are less than respectful
when they reach out to other bloggers?**

Yes, and I don't know what it is. Maybe it's something about the Internet, because I don't run into people like this too often on the street. Sometimes, people will email you and expect that you'll jump for them. That doesn't show much respect. But if someone is more humble and respectful in their approach, I'll certainly appreciate that.

**Do you have any other, more specific advice
for aspiring political bloggers?**

It's important to proofread your writing as much as possible and avoid spelling errors. Nobody's impressed with someone who sounds stupid.

**Are there certain things you wish less experienced
political bloggers would do differently?**

Yes, I don't want to sit and read three or four page postings. I want to see it and get it within a short amount of time. So people who write postings that are like novels don't interest me. I just don't have the time.

Another thing is that a lot of new bloggers write about how they feel, and they tend to get all sappy. I don't really care about that. I just want to know what happened. I just want to get the facts.

Briefly put, how has the political blogosphere changed over time?

What's different today, as I mentioned earlier, is that anybody can put up videos, and that it's easy. That's changing our whole society. When you have a video out on the Internet, the news media are going to report on it. They have to. When people see a video, it's so much more of a story than if they just read about it. It's more believable to people. It's just amazing. You notice it with your hits that, when you have a story with video, it gets a lot more attention.

Another thing is the rise of *Twitter*, which I've started using more recently. It can help you find some good stories, because everybody's on *Twitter*.

The media have stopped ignoring bloggers. In fact, most media have their own blogs today, like the *National Review*'s "The Corner." It's been a great move for that organization. If you have an organization, you need to have a blog. It's going to draw in people, readership, and help build a community.

13
Steve Clemons

While some of the world's top political bloggers entered the political blogosphere with little more than a passion for politics, others have come to it with a lifetime's worth of high-level policy experience. Steve Clemons, who runs *The Washington Note* for the New America Foundation, a nonpartisan public policy think tank, clearly falls in that second category.

Prior to joining the New America Foundation, where he directs its American Strategy Program, Clemons served as Executive Vice President of the Economic Strategy Institute, Senior Policy Advisor on Economic and International Affairs to Democratic Senator Jeff Bingaman, Executive Director of the Nixon Center, co-founder and Director of the Japan Policy Research Institute, and the Executive Director of the Japan-America Society of Southern California, among other positions. In addition to working for the New America Foundation, Clemons is Managing Director of the Washington, D.C. office of Fenton, the largest public interest communications firm in the U.S.

Why would a political insider like Clemons — whose writings appear in the world's leading newspapers and magazines, is a guest on many of the major television and radio news shows, and who regularly socializes with senators, ambassadors and other political dignitaries — feel the need to blog? The answer is simple. For Clemons, as for the other individuals profiled in this book, blogging offers the means to express his views in a timely and effective manner, and in a way that's not dependent on the prior approval of what he refers to as a "cartel of editors." It serves, in a word, as Clemons's very own op-ed page. Indeed, Clemons sees blogging as one of several forms of writing that budding policy analysts need to be able to master. To that end, the interns who work for him at the New America Foundation all contribute to the blog; a feature which both serve to further hone their professional skills and helps broaden the range of issues covered by the blog.

As a political insider with numerous high-level contacts, Clemons has broken many important stories over the years, including President Obama's appointment of Hillary Clinton as his Secretary of State and appointment of James Smith as his Ambassador to Saudi Arabia. He's most widely known, however, for his blogging about former Undersecretary of State John Bolton's 2005 bid to become the U.S. Ambassador to the United Nations. Clemons's sustained coverage is credited with helping to galvanize public opinion against Bolton which, in turn, contributed to the Senate's subsequent failure to support his nomination. *Time Magazine* has named *The Washington Note* one of the "Best Blogs" in recognition of these and other accomplishments.

#####

When and why did you start *The Washington Note*?

I started *The Washington Note* a little over seven years ago. I'd been encouraged to do so for the previous two years by Joshua Marshall from *Talking Points Memo*, a friend of whom eventually helped me design the blog.

I work at a think tank, the New America Foundation. While our think tank is a relatively new one, we quickly became very dominant in the op-ed pages. We were publishing in *The New York Times*, *The Washington Post*, and various other places. I didn't like that we were always subject to this control by a cartel of editors and thought that there must be a faster and better way. So I started the blog because I wanted to move material into online print more quickly, and in a way in which I could dominate a subject and not be dependent on an editor.

I began blogging about foreign policy issues that concerned me and, when the John Bolton issue came along, I thought about it very carefully. George Bush had beaten John Kerry in 2004 and, in early 2005, he nominated John Bolton for the UN. It was a huge issue for me.

I thought to myself, "Wow, I know a lot about Bolton and his situation is more fragile than people realize. If you leave it to the mainstream media, they'll never cover this right." So I started the Bolton battle at a time when no one thought it was a big deal.

To sum it up, I started blogging for very practical reasons, to rectify what I saw as deficiencies in other areas.

What was the experience like when you first started out?

When I first started out, I didn't know very much about blogs, readers, and the scale of readership. During the 2004 presidential election, I was sent a flier saying that the Democrats would ban the Bible and turn their states into baskets of homosexuality.

This flyer was going to church parishes in Kentucky, West Virginia, Arkansas and Ohio. Someone sent it to me, and I put it on the blog. Next thing I knew *CBS News*, Howard Dean, John Kerry and John Edwards were all speaking about this, and I got enormous traffic. It also brought in a lot of people who wanted to support the blog.

You are the primary blogger on *The Washington Note*. Why did you decide to bring on a number of co-bloggers?

I'm the primary blogger, and I've been that from the very beginning. Most of the people I've brought in already worked for me. They are interns. I believe that anyone who works in my group at the New America Foundation needs to learn how to write. They need to learn to think and communicate.

I also want them to be able to communicate in multiple forms. They should be able to write briefs as well as blog posts. And they've a diverse set of interests that are much wider than mine.

So I also brought them in because I could have someone who could write about Latin America, Turkey or other issues that just don't interest me that much. It broadens the scope of issues and it gives them professional opportunities.

What are your goals for the site?

My blog is designed to think through the strategic choices for the U.S. It was designed to be a response to the neo-conservatives and, to some degree, liberal interventionists who didn't realize that American military, economic, and moral power had been deflated significantly. They continue to act as if this isn't the case.

I found that the old-line liberal interventionists had done very little to replenish their ranks and very little to compete intellectually with what the neo-conservatives were doing. So, partly, what I wanted to do was to offer smart thinking about strategic choices.

Another part of it is slightly more personal. I go to a lot of parties in Washington, D.C. I talk to ambassadors, Senators and their staff people, and I realized from watching TV shows like *The West Wing* that there's a huge interest among the American public in this kind stuff but very few portals for them to look into it. So I decided to also give them a little bit of a personal feel of what's going on in his weird town.

**What role do you see *The Washington Note* playing
in the political sphere more generally?**

My blog is about showing the nuances, the different sets of views. I want to show people that political issues aren't simply partisan divides between Democrats and Republicans. They're partisan divides over how you look at the world and America's role in the world.

The Washington Note plays an important role as both a place of record and as a political instigator. It's like my own op-ed page as well as a space for serious analysis of what I think is interesting. It's opinion journalism, but it's opinion journalism designed to have a political impact. It combines analysis, opinion-making and advocacy in ways that the mainstream media don't.

How do you decide what to blog about on any given day?

I always have two tiers going on simultaneously. I have one tier of things that I'm thinking about but can't get to right away. I don't like bloggers who always respond immediately. Sometimes I need to think things over. I throw them in a file, and that's sort of my think file.

Then there's stuff like the ongoing U.S.–China dialogue. Those are pieces that usually take me some time to write. It's the same with the Israeli–Palestinian peace process. What are the interlocking pieces in the region? Where does Syria fit in? How does all this work, and how do you explain it to people who're very dug in ideologically with one position or another?

I get about 1,000 emails a day, so I've got people constantly pitching me and trying to move stuff. I've a gusher of information, so I only go with what's interesting to me, where my head is.

Who is the blog aimed at?

I care about whether people in Washington, D.C., at the State Department, the Hill, and the White House are reading it. My target is an elite audience. And it is very read among elites. So, sometimes, writing a "who did what to whom story" helps drive the traffic.

**Aside from what you've already mentioned, do you do anything
in particular to attract that elite audience?**

Not really. Occasionally I'll put up pictures of my dog. It gives a human dimension to the blog. I've a long list of people who're addicted to the dog pictures. It kind of gives readers a view from my window. If you search under the name Oakley, you'll find millions.

What qualities do you most admire in a political blog?

Non-derivative thinking and analysis, that the person isn't just echoing or stealing someone else's thoughts. I like to see the quality of someone's original thinking and analysis, something that's unique. There are people out there who're able to do that regularly, like John Aravosis of *AMERICAblog* and Joshua Marshall of *Talking Points Memo*.

Another thing is that I tend to get bored very rapidly with predictability. I think bloggers ought to challenge their own biases. Sometimes I do that with guest-bloggers. I'll invite people I disagree with to guest-blog, and I also organize debates between different people on my blog.

Aside from organizing debates between different people, do you do anything else to make *The Washington Note* stand apart in the political blogosphere?

I do some video. I occasionally include video with people that no one else does.

Why do you think you've been so successful?

I think it's because I'm wrestling with issues, wrestling with them as honestly as I can, that are important to people. I also think it's because I'm honest about the fact that I struggle, and because I've commenters. Some of them are outrageous. But, on the whole, they're smart. They're smart, outrageous, and passionate. And they often disagree with me. I allow that disagreement to thrive on my blog. In fact, I've people who read the commenters and not me. So I think that adds a lot to it.

I also beat the mainstream media by five days on the news that Hillary Clinton was going to be the new Secretary of State. And I was the first person to have the news on who'd be the new Saudi Ambassador. Stuff like that has positioned me as an insider that people don't need to read every day, but that they can't completely ignore.

Finally, people in the mainstream media read my blog all the time, and I'm a regular guest on many of the major news talk shows. That always drives traffic.

What advice would you give someone who wants to launch a political blog himself?

It really depends on the person. If it's a regular person off the street, I'd tell the person to go to a free site and try to find their voice. See if you've anything to say that's unique, show it to some people, and see if it sticks with any of them.

If it's a more serious player, I'd tell him or her to consider how to stand apart in a crowded marketplace. The person would then need to learn what other bloggers are doing in his or her particular area.

What mistakes do less experienced political bloggers tend to make?

I think that less experienced bloggers tend to spin out of control over silly things, and, sometimes, they confuse passion and emotion with analysis. Bloggers have to be thinkers. But a lot of the political blogosphere is based upon overstatement, hyperbole, attack.

Another problem is that new bloggers often feel they have to be out there all the time, so they quickly outrun their span of knowledge. They read something quickly, think they know it, and end up creating a small disaster. That undermines their credibility and makes them look trivial. So looking trivial, I think, undermines a lot of new bloggers.

How, in your mind, has the political blogosphere evolved over time?

In the beginning there weren't a lot of players. And we're still feeling our way forward in terms of what blogs are becoming. The big, well read, influential, political blogs are being bought up by mainstream media or, like Josh Marshall's blog, *Talking Points Memo*, becoming conglomerates in their own right.

So they're either sizing up or merging into other institutions. Market forces are driving the bigger, better blogs to become part of larger operations and networks.

There's a stratification going on right now whereby some people have big pipes and lots of people have small pipes. And, just like in the beginning, those that are small are very dependent on the bigger ones for attention. The smaller ones can move up in the hierarchy, though, if they find a niche or an issue that no one else is covering.

So the key, if you're just starting out as a political blogger, is to find you own, particular niche?

Yes. You need a small niche issue that's very interesting, but that nobody else is covering. When you become better known, you can branch into other issues.

14
Ben Smith

Ben Smith, who writes a blog bearing his own name for the political website *POLITICO*, is one of many people who've successfully made the transition from newspaper reporting to political blogging. After graduating from college in 2004, Smith worked as a political reporter for the *New York Observer* and the *New York Sun* and, subsequently, as a political columnist for the *New York Daily News*. During that time (2004–2006), he also launched three of New York City's leading political blogs, *The Politicker*, *Daily Politics*, and *Room Eight*, for which he still blogs occasionally about local New York City politics. Due to the successes of his blogs, *POLITICO* invited him in 2007 to start a blog that would focus on national politics.

Smith left the newspaper business and joined *POLITICO*, in large part, because he was unhappy with prevailing news reporting conventions. Much like Andrew Malcolm of the *Los Angeles Times*'s *Top of the Ticket*, who'd become increasingly disillusioned with what he calls "the girdled format of newspaper writing," Smith felt that the formal structure of news reporting — the inverted pyramid structure, the idea of balance — made it difficult for him to truly connect with readers. Blogging, on the other hand, has allowed Smith to connect more intimately with readers, both in the sense of soliciting critical feedback on his postings and ideas for future ones.

While Smith is critical of prevailing news reporting conventions, it's important for him to uphold the traditional distinction between reporting and commenting when he blogs. Unlike most of the other political bloggers profiled in this book, Smith is wary of infusing his blogging with his own personal opinions. He's well-known both within and outside the political blogosphere for his hard-hitting, original reporting. During the 2008 presidential election, Smith broke the story about Barack Obama's relationship with former Weatherman Bill Ayers, and provided some of the earliest reporting on the various conspiracy theories surrounding Obama's birth and religion. In 2010, he broke the story about a confidential Republican National Committee fundraising presentation which counseled the party to capitalize on the fear among people that Obama's policies would lead the U.S. along the path to socialism.

What inspired you to start blogging?

After college, I worked for the *New York Sun* covering City Hall and then for the *New York Observer*. At that time, during the 2004 elections, I also started reading blogs. The *New York Observer* is a weekly publication, so I'd all this information that I couldn't use because it wasn't big enough for a weekly news article. It also struck me as a good way to ease the frustrations of working for a weekly publication.

Right after the 2004 elections, I started one up myself on *Blogger*. I did it really informally, didn't tell my bosses about it. I only told a few friends and sources to take a look at it and see what they thought. It took off very fast. My blog, *The Politicker*, was the first New York political blog, which was incredibly fun because I'd the whole landscape to myself. Everybody was just frantically hitting the "refresh" button on it all day.

Then I left the *New York Observer* and went to the *Daily News* and started a competing blog as well as a sort of diary-based group blog. I subsequently went to work for *POLITICO* in the beginning of 2007. They were hiring people just before they launched and were looking for a very aggressive, newsie, and fact-based blog. Not a lot of people were doing this and, since I was one of the few, they hired me to do it.

Has the blogging format been a natural fit for you?

Yes, it totally suits my metabolism. I've always been the kind of reporter who likes to write a piece, get it done, and then never to want to see it again. Blogging takes the instant gratification of reporting to a new height.

I've always felt a little dissatisfied with newspaper reporting. You master the form, the pyramid structure, the idea of balance, the formal structure of it. But it's quite hard to do it in a way that connects very intensely with your readers. And there's no channel for feedback. It's tough.

My very partisan editor of the *New York Sun*, Seth Lipsky, was a master of writing stuff that really inflamed people, that felt very immediate, and that pushed the buttons very hard. But it's a hard thing to do. You often feel that you're just producing a product that's of this shape and that size, but that it doesn't connect with readers. Blogging, on the other hand, connects so immediately with readers. You can't get away with any bullshit, because you're called on it instantly.

It's a very two-way street. The email tips are just the best thing. You're constantly tapping into this rich vein of suggestions and facts. There's nothing like it.

Do you still look at yourself as a straight reporter when you blog?

I do. Once in a while, I sit on panels of bloggers. So I think the term is sort of in the way. It's so wedded to a particular form when the different forms are, in fact, blurring. The differences are getting more subtle and the platforms are getting more sophisticated although, of course, blogging does have certain, particular qualities, like the use of first-person.

**So blogging has allowed for an expanded notion
of what straight reporting entails?**

Yes, although I've always felt that there's a line between sensibility and opinion, and this is something the *New York Observer* has been very good at upholding. As a straight reporter, you're entitled to your sensibility. That's your kind of opinion. That's the line I try to keep in mind when I blog.

On that note, what are you trying to achieve journalistically speaking?

It's very reader-driven. It's about answering people's questions and continuing a conversation that's interesting to readers. And, of course, that often matches up with the traditional journalistic goals of exposing truths and telling people what's going on.

Politics is particularly well suited to blogging, because politics has always had this fabric of gossip and personality stuff that weaves it all together, although people sometimes sneer at it. It's always been incredibly important to the fabric of it. Blogging isn't so much a vehicle for covering politics as it's a place where it takes place.

How do you decide what to blog about on any given day?

I don't really feel like I decide what to cover. Rather, I sort of choose what not to blog about. I'm probably as plugged into the stories of the day as anybody, the stuff that's new, the stuff that adds to the sum of information for people who're paying a great deal of attention to politics. It's really about advancing the story, broadly speaking.

Who do you blog for?

I definitely blog for people who're paying total attention to politics and who are, in their own minds, on a first name basis with most of the players. It's certainly also written to be consumed by the people who're the actual players in the stories I cover.

My readers tend to be younger, highly educated, political junkies and very often people who themselves have worked or work in politics. These are also the readers who send me the most email.

Do you actively seek out a younger audience?

Not really. The only audience I feel like I actually need is the insiders. I want the candidates themselves to call me and say, "What the hell if this?" That would be the ideal.

Do you do anything in particular to attract and retain readers?

I actively use stuff forwarded to me from readers. And when I do it, I make clear whether I dipped into the comments section or whether it was from an email, or both. That way, you engage more with readers and relate to them more as equals.

What makes for a high-quality political blog in your opinion?

The most important thing is that it's a place where you can get information that's not available elsewhere. Another thing that's required, of course, is a certain degree of sophistication. You have to be part of the larger conversation, and you have to be aware of what the conversation is about. It has to be about the very highest level of decision-making. In fact, it has to be about stuff that White House officials, who're deeply involved in it, will immediately recognize as being plugged in.

Do you do anything in particular to ensure that your blog stands apart in the political blogosphere more generally?

I try to break news every day. I also think that aggregation is really important and valuable, so I do a lot of that. But if there's no original reporting, it's a much less valuable thing, at least for what I do. There are other blogs that are just aggregation and commentary and do a great job.

Why do you think you've been so successful?

I think it's because I've figured out a New York kind of formula for covering campaigns in a very minute but not uncritical or unsophisticated way. It's a model that has worked well with what *POLITICO* is doing in terms of paying a great deal of attention to the presidential election.

I remember telling my bosses, when I first started out, that my blog was getting about 5,000 hits a day, which I thought was great. I told them I thought I could at least triple that with a national blog just because there's a larger circle of operatives. But, of course, I've more than tripled that. I've increased it more than ten-fold and, during the presidential election, way more on a good day. There was this tremendous interest in the campaign, and the stuff that previously would've been considered insider coverage became news by any journalistic standard.

What advice would you give people who want to give political blogging a try themselves?

It actually happens all the time. I always tell people that I'm not going to be interested in their blogging unless it's something that they know something about. I don't particularly care about your opinion of President Obama. Why should I?

But if you know something about U.S.–Canada relations, I'd tell you to start a blog about that. Maybe I can learn something from it. And if you every once in a while break some news, you're going to have something that's really valuable.

It's like that old newspaper saying, "Opinions are cheap but facts are expensive," which happens to be how newspapers pay. Reporters get salaries, while columnists get 200 dollars a pop. There's a real hunger and demand for information, but there's a glut of opinions.

So you'd encourage aspiring political bloggers to specialize in particular topics?

Absolutely, although the best bloggers defy that and tend to be very broad in scope. But a good beat is valuable in itself.

Are there certain mistakes that less experienced political bloggers commonly make?

Yes. The most boring thing in the world is to read at 4pm whatever talking points the Democratic and Republic National Committees put out at 10am and have already been filtered through the blogs: to get the second or third ripple on what has already happened.

So the main mistake is repeating what other bloggers have already covered?

Yes. There's too much echoing of whatever the partisan talking point of the day is. And lots of people talk about stuff they know nothing about.

Briefly put, what trends do you see with respect to political blogging?

The main thing is that it's beginning to merge with what used to be called the traditional media. It's already difficult to tell them apart. Ultimately, I think, there's not going to be such a thing as the political blogosphere. All journalism will be online.

There'll be a spectrum of facts and opinion, and people will come to it from different backgrounds. Some will have gone to journalism school and some won't. It won't be possible for the average reader as well as an honest expert to systematize the difference between the blogosphere and everywhere else.

So you expect to see a lot more fluidity?

Absolutely. The good bloggers very quickly figured out that being reliable, honest, and transparent are incredibly valuable things to readers. And newspapers figured out that being responsive is also very valuable.

15
Matthew Yglesias

Some people launch political blogs in the hope that, one day, they'll land a "legitimate" job in the mainstream news media. That's never been the motivating drive for Matthew Yglesias who writes the blog, *Yglesias*, for the Center for American Progress, a liberal progressive think-tank. Unlike many people, who start writing online because they're unable to find employment in daily newspapers or weekly magazines, Yglesias always wanted to write for the Web. Indeed, he sees that commitment as one of the reasons for his success as a blogger.

Yglesias started blogging as a hobby back in 2002, while he was an undergraduate student at Harvard University. After graduating with a degree in philosophy, in 2003, Yglesias joined *The American Prospect* as a Writing Fellow and later a Staff Writer, as well as contributed to the magazine's group blog *TAPPED*. At the same time, Yglesias continued writing his own blog. From 2007–2008, his blog was hosted by another political magazine, *The Atlantic Monthly*, after which he joined the Center for American Progress where he's been ever since.

While blogging is Yglesias's main passion, he's also written for a number of prominent newspapers, including the *Guardian* and *The New York Times*, and has appeared on many television and radio shows as a political commentator. He's a regular contributor to *Bloggingheads.tv*, a video blog discussion site where the participants engage one another via webcam which is then broadcast online to viewers.

Aside from his genuine passion for blogging, Yglesias attributes his success to the fact that he blogs around the clock, engages his readers by responding to their emails and participating in the comment threads and, not least importantly, to the fact that he's become known for his coverage of a number of very specific issues (notably land use, transportation, and urban planning) in addition to his blogging about the more general political issues of the day.

#####

Why did you start blogging?

I started blogging quite a while ago, in January of 2002, when I was still a college student. I didn't have any particular motivation other than it seemed interesting. I was doing it for about a year, while some people I knew at different political magazines pointed to some entry-level positions available at the places where they worked.

I didn't know what I wanted to do with my life, so I applied for some of those positions. I was mostly turned down but one place, *The American Prospect*, wanted to hire me. I started to write for the magazine but was also contributing to a group blog that they had.

Then, after working there for about six months, they offered me a permanent position and a raise.

I accepted the position, and the following year the blogging phenomenon really started to take off. It began to become clear that being good at writing a blog was a skill that people would be looking for. I wrote some decent magazine articles but didn't feel I stood out in that field. Instead, I started to take blogging seriously as a permanent career.

What are you trying to achieve with your blogging?

I hope to be engaging people. I've a growing audience of people on issues that I think are important. I hope to increase their understanding of what's happening with those issues. But, to be honest, it's something I really enjoy doing. I started doing it as a hobby when I was a college student, with no particular expectation of accomplishing anything.

Initially, I did it for my own amusement. Now I also do it because I get paid a salary. But, ultimately, I'm hoping that people come to a better understanding of policy issues in the news.

**How does your blogging relate to your other work
at the Center for American Progress?**

The blog is a big part of the work that I do. In fact, everything I do at CAP is about trying to find innovative ways to communicate progressive ideas to the public. Some of that involves working with other people who're going to be spokespeople. Some of that involves strategizing about what we want to say. Some of it involves doing media appearances.

It's all about creating a political communication universe in which you try to make people see things the right way, trying to build support for good ideas. That's what the larger team I'm working with at CAP is doing.

Where do you get your inspiration from when you blog?

I've an RSS reader that follows certain blogs. That includes some of the highest-traffic blogs as well as a lot blogs that are written by academics. They don't necessarily have the best websites out there, but they have some good ideas that people aren't necessarily seeing elsewhere.

The first thing I do, when I get up in the morning, is scan the headlines from various news sites and the headlines from these experts and try to throw up some posts. Then I usually shift into reading the newspapers beyond the front-page headlines, to see if there are any interesting developments.

Over the course of the day, I catch new blog posts when they come up. I work with a team of colleagues who're constantly emailing around tidbits that they find. And a lot of my colleagues are really expert at seeing what's on radio shows, seeing what's going on in more obscure places.

I often have conversations with people or get emails from them about work they're doing or things they've seen. I've an audience of people who do work they want other people to see and therefore often bring their work to me. I put it up, have good contents, and people read it. It's a virtuous circle.

On that note, who's reading your blog?

It's an audience of people who're very interested in politics and political debate, who're interested in a level of detail and depth that doesn't exist in the regular newspapers or the general interest media. I know that readers from Washington, D.C., Maryland, and Virginia are over-represented relative to their population size. So it's a lot of people who're actually working professionally in politics.

Do you also try to reach journalists and policy-makers?

Increasingly, mainstream journalists have started to look to blogs as a way to take the temperature of what's going on. Some journalists are actually very passionate about the issues and like to read about them on blogs. I think that a lot of journalists working at newspapers like their jobs but have an interest in a certain level of richness that doesn't fit the format they're working in. They are interested in seeing what people have to say in a more analytical way.

I don't think many politicians are in the blog reading demographic, although you definitely get people who're working on the staff at the Hill. Some of the people I know working in the executive agencies, as well as the generation of people who's currently in their 20s and 30s and on the way to become the next elected official cohort, read blogs.

What do you do to retain readers?

The main thing I do is simply to be consistent. The blog is up all the time. There are posts on weekends. There are posts on Christmas Day. The idea is to discourage people from drifting away. If you give them a break, they might find that there's something else that's just as good, and they might go away.

The other thing I do is try to engage the audience. I don't respond to every email I get, but I respond to a lot of them. I also participate to some extent in the comment threads. I link back to bloggers who link to me. The point is to get people to feel involved in the project.

What do you consider the defining features of a high-quality political blog?

Frequency is very important. You get a lot of readers just from having a lot of stuff. You also have to cover the main stories of the day as well as have a healthy dose of material that's idiosyncratic to you and your site, material that isn't just the same as everyone else's.

Do you do anything in particular to ensure that your blog stands apart in the political blogosphere more generally?

There are a couple of issues which are identified with me and that aren't other people's issues. They mostly have to do with urban planning, land use, and transportation, although they're not the main focus of my blog by any stretch. But I blog about those issues a lot, as well as about health care, climate change, and transportation.

I also try to maintain a blog that's a little more personal and informal than other people's by blogging about issues that are a little bit more offbeat. It sets me apart from other people.

Why do you think your blog has been so successful?

I think the fortitude of timing has played a large role. I also think it has a lot to do with the fact that I really like doing it. I think that a lot of people who're writing on the Internet these days are people whose dreams in high school or college was to write long magazine articles. Because that sector of the industry hasn't been doing well, they've found themselves taking jobs writing on the Internet.

I don't think anyone could be a good feature magazine writer who didn't really want to be a feature magazine writer. And I think it's the same thing for blogging. At this point in time there are relatively few people who really like the idea of new media writing and writing for the Web. Part of the reason I hopped on it at the time was because it's something that really spoke to me in a way that other forms of writing hadn't. It's something I think I'm able to do well simply because I've a real passion for it. I don't see my job as a kind of second-best alternative or a stepping-stone to a different kind of job. It's exactly what I want to be doing.

What advice do you have for someone who wants to launch a political blog himself?

The main thing is that you have to do explicit outreach. You have to identify people, based on what you've read from their work, who might be interested in what you're doing. You have to get in touch with them, possibly with individual posts that comment on what they're doing or they might be interested in. The other thing is that, realistically speaking, there's strength in numbers. It might be advisable to get together with two, three, or four other people and do a group blog because that way you'll get more content up. You'll have more ability to reach out to people and just more ability to deliver consistency and build an audience over time.

Do you have any other, more specific advice for aspiring political bloggers?

Sure. It's especially important, in terms of quality, to ask why people would be reading it. What do you know that other bloggers don't know? What value is being provided? This is especially important if you're new and don't have an institution backing you. People are instinctively going to be a little bit wary. So you really have to find subjects you're knowledgeable about, and deliver information that, if other people link to you, they don't wind up looking like idiots.

I know that a lot of people will read a couple of blogs and decide that it looks easy. But it's not easy. So it's really worth thinking about it. What could I do? What level of interest do I have in this? How committed am I? What is it that I'm bringing to the table?

What is my unique contribution?

Exactly.

Are there certain mistakes that less experienced political bloggers are especially prone to make?

Yes. There's too much echoing of what more prominent bloggers are already saying. That's a problem. The other thing that I see people doing all the time is simply giving up too quickly on sites that are actually fine. They don't realize that, by the nature of it, it takes a long time to build up an audience. In fact, if you've a site that any people are reading who don't know you personally, you're actually being fairly successful.

There are people who're interested in it, and if you keep up the work that those people are interested in, you'll get a growing audience. But it takes time. You have to make contact with that audience and see why they're interested. People will get discouraged because they have 500 readers and feel that that's not very many readers. But, essentially, it's a lot of people, considering that they care about you.

How, in your opinion, has the political blogosphere evolved over time?

In terms of coverage of big national issues, I think we're looking at more and more institutionalization and professionalization where, eventually, a fixed number of big sites will dominate. But I also think that we're set for a real explosion of local news and public affairs sites because that's the area in which the newspaper realm is retreating the fastest.

If someone wrote a really good news and public affairs blog about the greater Detroit area, the fact that that metro region now has a newspaper which doesn't even publish seven days a week would draw a lot of readers to it. And it becomes pretty obvious what value you might add relative to other people. You know what happened at the City Council meeting.

The first generation of bloggers were people who'd gotten interested in the most obvious political controversy: Do you think there's going to be a war in Iraq? But, in Washington, D.C., I see a lot of interesting neighborhood-oriented sites. I think that'll be the next, big growth in the blogging field.

So if someone wanted to launch a political blog tomorrow, you'd recommend that the person start a locally-based blog?

Yes, but it really depends on what you're trying to do. And it'd only work if you're really interested in it. I think that people will continue to start sites of various kinds. But we'll see that people who do reporting on local issues will find that there's a big niche for that. Yet, a lot of people will continue to want to do commentary on national issues. Some of them will do it well and become successful but they'll find that it's a very crowded space in which it's hard to break in, whereas someone who has a passion for understanding their city or town will find that they don't have much competition, and that people still care about what happens there.

So in terms of the future of political blogging, you imagine that we're going to see a bunch of big blogs like *The Huffington Post*, as well as many smaller, local blogs?

Yes, that would be my guess.

16
John Hawkins

John Hawkins of *Right Wing News* is one of many examples of how far sheer determination, will power, and hard work can catapult you in the political blogosphere. With few professional credentials, no high-powered political contacts, and limited journalistic experience, he's managed to create one of the most widely read and influential conservative blogs. From humble beginnings, Hawkins has gone on to interview a long roster of conservative luminaries on his site, including Ann Coulter, Tom Delay, Milton Friedman, Newt Gingrich, and Mike Huckabee. Due to his success as a political blogger, he's become a columnist for one of the premier conservative websites, *Townhall.com*, regularly appears on major radio shows, and has become so well-known that he charges thousands of dollars for his public appearances.

Over the past few years, Hawkins has taken his passion for politics beyond writing and speaking and into the realm of political advocacy and fundraising. He worked on former Republican congressman Duncan Hunter's presidential run in 2008 and sat on the board of Slatecard, an organization that raised more than half a million dollars for local Republican candidates. In 2006, he created and led a group of political bloggers called *Rightroots*, the first major fundraising effort on the conservative side of the political blogosphere which raised several hundred thousand dollars for Republican candidates.

Hawkins wasn't always such a prominent public figure. Prior to launching *Right Wing News* in 2001, his only journalistic experience had been writing for a small print-zine, an Internet gaming magazine, and running a small web-based humor magazine. When he was laid off from his job in 2005, he seized the opportunity to blog full-time, and he's done so ever since. In 2007, he started adding contributors to the site and now has more than a dozen co-bloggers.

#####

What inspired you to start blogging?

I'd been interested in writing for quite a long time. I used to work for a little print-zine in Charlotte, North Carolina called *Fubar*. Then I worked at a gaming magazine that, basically, showed people how to play a particular Internet game that I was good at. That's how I cut my teeth. From there I went to run a website called *Brass Knuckles Webzine*, which was mostly a humor magazine. A couple of thousand people viewed it a day, but then it kind of stalled.

When the 2000 presidential election came around, I'd lost interest in politics. I hadn't paid much attention to it, but got so infuriated watching what was happening. The key moment for me was watching the election returns come in. Bush, of course, had been ahead all along, but then I saw some caller on *CNN* saying, "Bush needs to concede."

I thought to myself, "Somebody needs to come out, speak out, and give conservatives a voice out there." That's what I wanted to do. That's when I stepped up. And that's how *Right Wing News* got started.

That was in 2001. In 2005, I got laid off from my job. At that point, I went full-time and have been blogging full-time ever since.

You were the only contributor in the beginning, right?

Yes, it was written entirely by me until 2007, when I started adding weekend bloggers. A couple of years ago, I turned it into a full-time group blog.

Why did you decide to do that?

Because there's only so much content you can pump out in a day. I looked at it and said to myself, "I'm pumping out six posts a day, which is a lot of content for one person. That's 3,000–4,000 words a day." But when I looked around, I saw that, compared to a lot of other bloggers, I was still not pushing out that much content. So I decided to get some more people on board.

Initially, I just asked a number of people from different sites if I could post their material on my blog. If I needed some content, I'd read maybe 20 blogs and, if I found something I liked, I'd post it on *Right Wing News* and link back to them.

Then I decided that I needed something more regular than that. So I started reaching out to various bloggers. There are a lot of talented people in the political blogosphere.

So that has been the major challenge?

Yes. The challenge has been to produce enough content, because I knew from the moment I started that I wanted to do it for a living. Nobody was doing it for a living back then. I think Andrew Sullivan of *The Daily Dish* was the only one.

Professionally, I was doing technical support at work, and the good thing about that, one of the reasons that I took this job, was that I could work on my blog at work. I also spent a lot of time working on it at home. I got to the point where I'd be doing my job, eat dinner, maybe work out, go back home, work until 3 or 4am, and then get up at 6 or 7am. I'd do that week after week, month after month, year after year.

So that was the real challenge. The challenge was finding the time and fitting it into my lifestyle. I'm a single guy, so it was a little easier for me. But it takes up an enormous amount of time.

Where do you look for inspiration for your postings?

The only thing that's fast enough for me is the Internet. I've over 120 blogs in my RSS reader, and I've a variety of different ones that I like to read on a daily basis. If you skim through a few of the certain ones, you'll know all the big issues of the day. Then you start to look for the smaller issues. That's how I keep informed. It's very Internet-based.

I also listen to talk radio. I listen to Rush Limbaugh. I listen to Tammy Bruce. I occasionally watch cable news, but I don't watch any of the shows regularly. I don't touch newspapers because they're usually two or three days behind what I've read on the Web already.

You mentioned earlier that *Right Wing News* was born out of your frustration during the 2000 presidential election. Moving forward, why do you continue to blog?

I blog because I want to become a political rock star in conservative circles. I want to be Ann Coulter. I want to be Thomas Sowell. I want to be someone like that. I want to have the books. I want to have the columns. I want to have everybody know my name. I want people to know who I am when I go on a television or radio show. I want to make a difference. I'm in this because I think the country needs people like me doing what I do.

I think that what I'm doing is extremely important. I think it's very important to have people doing what I'm doing for the country. That's how I look at it.

What do you do to become a political rock star?

I generate traffic. If you want to become a political rock star, it's all about getting people to want to read you and getting out in front of people on a daily basis. I spend a lot of time in front of a computer screen. I have to. I spend a lot of time hitting a lot of different websites.

I also do radio shows all the time. Let me give you an example. If someone offers me to come on a radio show at 7am, I'll get up 30 minutes before, do the show, and then go back to bed. I'll do that.

You have to be immersed in it, and you have to stay immersed. That's how you get good at anything, whether it's basketball, science, or blogging. You get in it, you get deep in it, and you stay in it all the time.

Who're you trying to reach with your blog?

The short answer: Conservatives. The same audience as Rush Limbaugh. There are also big-name journalists who read me. But my target audience is conservatives. That's what I'm shooting for. That's as deep as it gets. I'm looking for the average conservative, although most of the people who read blogs are more politically active. Something like 90% of my readers vote. 75% of them have gone to Tea Parties.

So these are politically active people. They're more intelligent than the average person. The average person who reads blogs is a little bit more intelligent than the person who just watches television. And, as a general rule, they tend to be a little more affluent.

Do you do anything in particular to attract and retain those readers?

To me, it's simply a matter of trying to put in the best quality work that I can and trying to get a quality staple of guest-bloggers. The good thing about having all these guest-bloggers is that they don't all write about the same issue. So, in the course of the day, we've enough people to pretty much hit all the big issues, the ones everybody's talking about. So you can get a good feel for what's going on by reading *Right Wing News*.

More generally, what would you say are the defining features of a high-quality political blog?

It's got to have a large amount of content. That's important. It's also got to be well-written. That's important. And all the best of the best have something unique about them. You can always go out, if you think about it enough, and find something that the best blogs do better than anybody else. *Atlas Shrugs*, for instance, covers radical Islam better than anybody else. *Power Line* broke the Rathergate story. Every one of them, if you go down the list and break it down, has something unique that they do.

What do you do to distinguish *Right Wing News* from all the other political blogs out there?

I look at myself as a sort of cleanup hitter, so I try to do stuff that's going to pull in traffic. I like to have at least one big post that I think has the potential to draw traffic each day. I've a lot of sources in Congress, so I can pull out material there. I used to do more but do a little less now, because I think I can put more time into it. I can improve the quality of writing and give the other bloggers a chance to pull in traffic, because I try to do unique material.

I also do a lot of interviews with famous people, like Ann Coulter and Michelle Malkin. I've done interviews with Milton Freeman.

What do you think has been the key to the success of *Right Wing News*?

I don't think I can boil it down to one thing. I think I've a talent for it. It's no different than, say, basketball. You've got to have a talent for it. You've got to have some ability. Two, you've got to work hard. I've worked like a dog on this.

Nobody can ever look at me and say, "Oh, you got handed this." I didn't know anybody in politics when I first started out. I'd no contacts. So you've got to really work hard. You've got to keep going.

It took me a while, too. Keep in mind that I've been doing this for ten years now. It took me a full four years to get to the point where I was able to do it full-time. And that's four years of working like it was a full-time job, a second full-time job, even when I wasn't getting paid very much money for it.

Aside from what you've already mentioned, what advice do you have for people who want to try to emulate your success?

I'd tell people to focus on something very specific like, say, global warming. Choose a topic that you're interested in, that you can write a lot about, and that you can be better at than everybody else. Don't try to compete with 5,000 other bloggers who're already running similar sites.

So if someone wants to start a political blog, I'd tell them to find a specialty. Don't try to come out and do a general blog. You need to find your own little niche, kill that niche, do it better than anybody else, and continually put out good content. That's how you can advance a little faster.

Do you have any advice about how people should go about promoting their sites?

One thing I tell people, and you'd be surprised at how many people don't do this, is to pop off two or three days' worth of content first. When somebody comes over to your blog, you don't want them to come over and say, "Okay, they did a post last Tuesday, and there's one from this Friday." If you want to be a successful blogger, you've got to do a large amount of work. You've got to do a consistent amount of work. If you're not doing that, you're not going to be successful.

And some people, honest to God, will send you links to stuff that doesn't work on their page. You click on the page, and there's nothing there. So go out, do a few days' worth of content, and make sure it's stuff that's pretty good. Have one article that people are going to be super interested in, and start sending it out.

You might say, "Hey, my name is so-and-so with this new blog. Here's this fantastic article you're going to be interested in. It would be great, since I've a brand new blog, if you could shoot a little attention my way." That's a good way to do it. So many new bloggers send me stuff, and it's amazing to me how many of them aren't doing even the most basic level of work they'd need to do to become successful.

Aside from posting too infrequently, have you noticed any other mistakes that less experienced political bloggers commonly make?

Yes. New bloggers will often take the latest story on the *Drudge Report*, write up a post about it, perhaps 50 words, and then they'll send me a link to the story and their brief comment. I ask myself, "Why?" There are 500 people writing about that already.

It's okay to do that if it's supposed be a filler on their blog but, if you're going to send me a promo on something and ask me to go over and read your blog, for God's sake have something on there that I'm going to be interested in. Something I'll go look at and say, "Yeah, that's pretty good."

Don't send me over to your blog if it's junk. People do that all the time, I guess, because they don't really know what else to do. I send out promos, and I send out promos to more than 260 bloggers when I do it. I know more bloggers than anybody else. But when I send out promos, it's for something unique.

I wish other people would do the same thing. On an average day, I probably get 150 emails. It's tough to go through all of them, although I try to look at them. But, man, I don't like getting stuff that's junk. So you've got to think about that when you're trying to get other people's attention.

How has the political blogosphere changed since you started blogging?

It's gotten more commercial. When I started out, there really wasn't much of a way to make money. Blog ads have helped a lot with that. It's also gotten more professional in that you've got more big-name bloggers, more journalists, involved.

I also think that the level of quality, not surprisingly, has improved over time. I can personally tell you that I'm a much better writer than I was when I first started blogging. That's not surprising. When you write every day for ten years, you're going to get better at it. And I've got a lot of good bloggers writing for me. So *Right Wing News* has become a much better blog.

As far as trends go, the right dominated the Internet during the 1990s, the Clinton years. When Bush came to power, it slowly but surely turned to the left. The left got much bigger than the right. I think that's going to turn again. I expect that, while Obama is in office, the left will level off and the blogs on the right will take off.

So far, I haven't seen that happen. It looks like both the right and the left are growing at the moment. I think that has to do with the fact that Obama has a really big agenda. Once he slows down, which is definitely going to happen next year, I think you're going to see a lot more energy on the right, a lot more people coming online. And the left, I think, is going to slow down. So I think it's going to be the right, not the left, that's going to grow over the next few years.

I also expect to see a lot more buyouts of blogs. If you're a newspaper, it'd make much more sense to get someone who already has, say, 15-20,000 readers than to get a 27-year old intern and call him your new blogger, or to get someone from the newsroom that you're getting ready to lay off. You've got bloggers who've proven themselves, so why not go with them, especially since they can bring readers over to you.

17
Heather Parton

One of the biggest secrets in the political blogosphere was revealed on June 19, 2007 when "Digby," the pseudonymous author of the widely admired liberal blog *Hullaballoo*, accepted the prestigious Paul Wellstone Citizen Leadership Award, named in honor of the late Democratic Senator from Minnesota, at a major blogging convention in Washington, D.C. By accepting the award in person, Digby revealed that she wasn't, as most of her fellow bloggers and readers had assumed, a young man, but a middle-aged woman by the name of Heather Parton.

Unlike some people, who choose to blog pseudonymously out of fear that expressing their political views in public could damage them personally or professionally, Parton made her decision for philosophical reasons. A long-time critic of the increasing credentialism of American public life, Parton wanted to blog about politics from an absolute position of ideas rather than to establish her authority through her particular, professional credentials, age, and gender. Parton very much enjoyed the challenge, finding it intellectually stimulating and an act of discipline on her part to think through and articulate her views without relying on any specific personal authority.

Interestingly, Parton found the assumption that she was a man to make the greatest difference to her fellow bloggers and readers. Although she'd never meant to make other people believe this was the case, the assumption automatically granted her a lot of authority. When she revealed that she was, in fact, a woman, a lot of people re-evaluated what she'd written.

While Parton revealed her true identity several years ago, she did so reluctantly and continues to blog under her pseudonym. To this day, she's only made public a few details about her own background. Parton worked for a while for the Trans-Alaska Pipeline System during which time she went to radiographer school to learn how to read pipe x-rays. Subsequently, she graduated from the film school at San Francisco State University and moved to Los Angeles where she's worked for a number of major production companies, including Artisan Entertainment, Island Pictures, and Polygram.

A self-described political junkie, Parton's forays into political blogging began in the late 1990s when she was a regular contributor to several online political discussion forums. When a fellow contributor by the name of Duncan Black launched his own blog, *Eschaton*, Parton started commenting on his site. Black found her comments to be so insightful that he often featured them on the front page, and other readers were so impressed that they encouraged her to launch her own blog, which she did on January 1, 2003 — four and a half years before she revealed her identity.

What was your road to blogging like?

I started writing online back in the late 1990s and, mostly, I gravitated toward politics. It was an exciting but also a very frustrating time for a liberal Democrat like me. I found these communities online all over the world whom I could communicate with, exchange ideas, commiserate, validate.

That was very exciting to me. I've always been a political junky, but it's always sort of a random thing to find people who think as you do or, even if they don't, think about politics with the same intensity as you do. That's what I found online; everybody was there voluntarily and spending their time communicating with strangers. It was a very exciting thing, and I was drawn into it almost by instinct.

I literally couldn't help myself. It was something that was beyond my control. I'm not a technology person, but the Internet was like magic to me. From the minute it became available, I was intensely into it. So my blogging grew out of that. As I was blogging in these communities, I gained a reputation for writing commentary, and people seemed to like what I was doing.

I'd not intended to do anything other than just communicate with fellow political junkies on a casual basis. But blogging became quite a thing. It was after the presidential election in 2000 when things really heated up, and then in the run up to the Iraq war everything exploded online. Blogging, at that point, was dominated by conservatives or, rather, libertarians.

There weren't a lot of liberal blogs out there. And those of us who were involved in the blogging community were a fairly tight group. I was encouraged to start my own blog, and that's what I did. Because it was a fairly tight community, it took off pretty quickly. Many people already knew me from commenting on other blogs in these communities. So that's how it got started, and then it just grew exponentially. It's been a very interesting period in politics. It's sort of serendipitous that the whole thing came together at this same moment, and somebody like me jumped in and found my voice.

**You mentioned that you weren't particularly tech savvy.
How has it been to write in a blog format?**

The format has been totally natural. For whatever reason I found it to be an interesting form of writing. It's developed its own form over time, and everybody does it in their own way. But the feedback was what was really unique. Writers usually write in a vacuum. So having this community feedback was very gratifying. What it did to someone like me, and probably others as well, was to give the encouragement I needed early on to keep going. I don't know if I'd have been able to go on if I'd just been speaking into the void, if I just had been writing for myself or even for a small, discreet group of people.

The format and the writing part were surprisingly easy for me. I've written my whole life but not in this particular way.

The technology remains obscure, although the tools that they've created, like *Blogger* which I still write on, was really quite easy to use. So once I developed a very basic knowledge of HTML and learned enough to navigate the system, it was easy enough for me. That means it's really easy, because I'm at about a fourth grade level. In fact, I'm sure most fourth graders are far more competent than me. So the technology was actually a plus, because they had recognized how to make it user friendly. I was the perfect guinea pig for *Blogger*.

Why do you blog under your pseudonym, "Digby"?

I think most people think of me by my pseudonym, even people who know my name. So it's sort of an open secret. It's a funny thing, because I established my reputation as a blogger under that name. I guess it's the same thing with performers, or anybody who establishes themselves publically under a certain name. That's just how people know you. So when my real name came out, it was surprisingly uninteresting. No one really cared.

Really?

Yes. I'm sure people have googled me, but there's nothing to find. I've lived a very average life. There's nothing interesting about me. So, essentially, Digby is my public persona, and everything that I've said under that name is far more interesting than anything I've ever said under my own name.

Is that the reason why you decided to blog pseudonymously?

That was part of it. I'd different reasons than a lot of people. A lot of people blog pseudonymously because they're concerned about airing their political voice publically in a way that could damage their professional or personal reputation in some way. I didn't have that concern. I worked in liberal Hollywood. No one cared. I wasn't threatened in any way.

And I've have always been very upfront about my politics in my personal life. To me, it was more a matter of wanting to write and think out loud about politics in a sort of pure way. I've always been a critic of the credentialism of American life. It's part of my critique of politics and elitism in general. I've been writing about that for many years. And it's not that I come at this from any sense of personal resentment. I've had a successful life. I'm not complaining in any way that, gosh, I just can't get ahead.

That's just where my politics comes from. I've a sense of "small d" democracy that's very important to me. So what blogging and the anonymity of it offered was to come in and write about politics from an absolute position of ideas and not from class or from professional credentials, or even from age. Over time, though, I did reveal my age, but I didn't reveal my gender.

That was an interesting writing challenge, to write as a genderless entity. I found it to be very challenging intellectually and an exciting thing to do, because I'd to explain ideas without ever resorting to personal authority. I didn't exist as a person so everything that came out had to be vibrant and vivid but not personal.

I really enjoyed blogging pseudonymously and, as time went on, it became sort of second nature to me. I only revealed myself reluctantly. When it happened, I knew it was time. You can't go on like this forever. The world of blogging was changing, and we were all becoming more public personas. It'd gone from being a sort of clubby, little world to a more professional, activist endeavor. So I knew that I'd to do it, and I knew that it'd change things a little bit when I did. I'd established a reputation, so it didn't damage me, but it did change things a little bit.

How did it change things for you?

It was mostly the gender issue. I'd been given a lot of automatic authority with the assumption that I was male, and I never corrected that. There were plenty of people who thought I was female, too, but for the most part people assumed that I was male. And once you reveal your gender, a lot of people go back and reevaluate things you've said from that new perspective. "Oh, that was a woman saying that and not a man," they think to themselves.

So there was a period of mistrust, I think, where people felt a little duped. Some people liked it, and they were like, "Oh, that's so cool. I'd no idea you were a woman." Other people felt that, maybe, I'd been dishonest with them, although I'd never said anything. But it passed. It was a bit of a jolt at the time, but it passed. I never consciously set out to have people think of me as male, and I was very consciously writing without referring to gender. So I wasn't trying to fool anyone but, then again, I wasn't exactly being upfront either.

Looking back on it, it was as much an experiment as anything else. In fact, it was a great act of discipline for me as a blogger, because it forced me to think through my arguments in ways that I'd not have done otherwise — issues that I feel strongly about, like feminism and war. Blogging about these issues as a woman would have been different than blogging about them as Digby, this genderless identity.

So, looking back on it, I'm glad I did it. I think all writers should have that experience, because it's eye opening when you have to challenge your own assumptions all the time and figure out ways to talk about things without relying on your personal experience, your own life story.

You mentioned earlier that you were attracted to blogging because it offered a sense of community. What are you trying to do politically speaking?

I'm a pretty traditional liberal, although I've a strong civil libertarian side. So, in some respects, I suppose there are issues on which I'd disagree with some liberals. I just consider myself a citizen trying to make my world a better place. I'd very much like to see us come out of this era of movement conservatism that we've been in for the last 40 years and have a more tolerant, open-minded, liberal political system.

I actually believe that our society has been fairly liberal through this period. I think that, socially, there have been huge advances. So I'd like our political system to match society a little bit closer. To me, it's been almost like having parallel universes where political conservatism was on the rise at the same time as society was becoming more liberal. And I think part of the tension of the culture war is that it's politics versus life.

What role do you see your blog playing in the political sphere more generally? Do you see it as a grassroots effort, as a corrective to mainstream media, or perhaps as a space for analysis and discussion?

I'd say all of those things. I'm kind of a generalist. I don't specialize in any particular area. There are a certain number of issues that I'm personally interested in, but I follow current events quite closely. I even involve myself in grassroots and netroots activism. I also try to be a forum for ideas and discussion. I'm a strong media critic, and I work at that. One of my main objectives is to keep a close eye on the media and try to be a bit of a watchdog.

So I consider it to be all of those things. I'm hopeful that my blogging can be illuminating and, I suppose, if you asked me what the single most important thing that I do, I'd say that I try to analyze current events in politics and write about it in ways that are illuminating and entertaining. That's probably the best I can hope for.

How do you decide what to blog about on any given day?

Mostly it's kind of an "X-factor." I can be on a roll with a particular issue. I can roll with it for days on end and find various hooks to discuss that issue. Sometimes it's a conscious decision where I'm doing some netroots activism, so I want to focus the blog in a certain direction.

But that's not the way it normally works. I've certain issues that I follow closely but mostly, I think, it's led by events. I've my hobby horses. I think everybody does. And there are many times where I just decide that I've got to write about this. Something I came across, something that's totally outside of everybody else's interest at that moment, but that I feel I need to write about.

Most of the time, though, I'm driven by events. But I want to distinguish between events and the news cycle, because the news cycle sometimes is kind of phony and isn't really driven by the events that I believe are important. Sometimes the political blogosphere goes against the news cycle. We're actually finding a story line, a thread, that the mainstream media isn't following, or at least isn't following as closely as we are.

I don't always know what makes me want to blog about something. It's almost an emotional reaction, a thought-connecting exercise. I find something, some connection between what appears to be unrelated in some way, and something clicks and I recognize that there's an analysis there. I've just learned something, and I get the urge to share what I've learned. That's essentially it.

Who do you blog for? Do you primarily blog for a liberal audience, or do you also try to reach across the political divide? Are journalists and policy-makers also part of your audience?

I've to admit that, in many ways, most of us are preaching to the choir. I don't really think we're an outreach organization. But anyone is welcome. I've a very open policy of anybody wanting to comment on my blog, and I'm not particularly strict on that. In fact, many of my readers wish I was more restrictive. I'd say I'm probably speaking mostly to political junkies.

I know that journalists and policy-makers (or at least their staff) read my blog. I'm conscious of that, and certainly in my media criticism I'm conscious of journalists reading it.

But, for the most part, I try to reach political junkies. Those are the people who share this interest with me, who follow politics, and many of whom I assume are involved in one way or another. That's who I think about and am aiming for. I certainly am not aiming at persuading conservatives. That's just not part of my mission.

Do you do anything in particular to retain those readers?

The one thing I do now, but didn't use to do, is to make sure that I write on a regular, consistent basis. I've always written every day, but there were times when I'd only write one or two posts a day. Now I try to make sure that I write six to eight posts a day. That's a whole different thing. It's been a challenge for me to do that, because I'm kind of a slow writer.

I did that just by observing other blogs. I just went, "My God, these people are writing like crazy. I've got to keep up." Now my traffic is pretty stable, although I do get the sense that people drift in and out. And, certainly, the news cycle affects my traffic. That's one thing I'm aware of. If there's a big story happening, people want to come and find out what the bloggers are saying about what's going on.

But, in the normal course of things, my traffic has been pretty stable for years. I haven't really lost or gained a huge amount of traffic. I just seem to have a relatively solid base. I don't know if they're the same people. I've no way of telling if new people are replacing old ones.

So I just kind of let myself do what I do and hope it keeps working.

What, in your opinion, do the best political bloggers out there have in common?

The best political bloggers are really good synthesizers, able to synthesize in a few paragraphs an analysis that'll crystallize for people the essence of an issue. The best bloggers do that, and some of them are really terrific at it. It takes a particular talent to be able to synthesize five or six articles you read on an issue and bring it all together and provide the linkage. In fact, the purest form of bloggers are people who can get to the heart of the matter quickly, efficiently, and hopefully with some felicitous writing.

I go to bloggers who can tell me the story quickly and with a little attitude. I like bloggers like that. I'm not looking for somebody to just give me a straight "just the facts ma'am" thing. I'm looking for some attitude, even in a right-leaning blog.

There are also really good aggregators who're able to pull together important stories and put them all in one place for your attention. And, then, there's a whole end of blogging that's purely satire, and they're incredible. They're really some of the smartest, best bloggers out there, approaching blogging, and politics, and life from the perspective of humor. It's hugely valuable to what we're doing.

**On that note, what do you do to secure your
own place in the political blogosphere?**

I just do what I do. I'm not very self-conscious about it. I just write and hope that people come. So far, I've been lucky enough that people continue to read me. If, at some point, I find that I'm losing traffic, or that I'm becoming dramatically unpopular, perhaps I'll look at it. It's almost like I'm afraid to overanalyze what I do.

Why do you think your blog has been so successful?

I think the simple answer is that people like the way I write, that they find what I've to offer valuable. My blog isn't particularly fun. The interactivity is really crude. There's nothing about it that would make people come there, except for me.

I also have to mention that I've a couple of contributing writers that people like. I pick people who I think are good writers, and that nobody really knew before they came along here.

**What advice would you give someone who
wants to launch a political blog himself?**

The first thing I'd say is that you have to concentrate on the writing. Make sure that you think about what you're writing, and try to write it in an original and interesting voice. Assuming that you feel you've done that, then you have to think about ways to get that voice out there. It's a difficult thing, but there are ways that you can do it. You have to scope out the bloggers who write about the things that you're interested in and try to get them interested.

Linkage is a very important part of blogging. Linking back and forth can bring awareness. You need to spend a lot of time commenting on other people's blogs, establishing your voice there, and not just use it as an opportunity to throw your link into the comments. Really engage with the community, because it's a community, and people talk back and forth. If you become someone in the comment section that people value, they'll check out your own blog.

It's sort of a relentless, yet subtle, attempt to get people to notice what you're doing. There's a community there. You know who your audience is. So, in that sense, it's a lot easier than trying to sell some other product. You know exactly where to find these people. You just have to do it in a way that isn't obnoxious and is bringing something valuable to the table.

If you're somebody like me who's a political junkie and does this out of an interest in politics, then you're going to have to bring something special to the table in terms of either what you write about or how you write about it. So you probably have to think a lot about the writing, and make sure that you're writing something that stands out.

It's very difficult not to crack, but people succeed. Every year somebody new comes along and breaks through.

Have you noticed any mistakes common to less experienced political bloggers?

The mistake that new bloggers often make is to try to recreate an established blog, writing about the same issues and throwing in their comments saying "Look what's happening in Iran. Boy, that's something." They're basically replicating what they've seen as being successful. The problem is that there are so many blogs that those formulas don't work with a new blog. You have to invent a new kind of blog in order to be successful, and people do that. They either find a niche that was unfilled, or they somehow capture people's imagination and begin to gather an audience. You really have to try and come at it from a new angle.

How has the political blogosphere changed since you started blogging?

It's changed a lot. In the beginning, it was basically a community and an ongoing conversation. It's still that, but it's become much more. It's now a major, political organizing tool. And it's become a voice for people outside the political system. A formidable voice. I don't know that we've changed the world, but we certainly have influence.

I'm not just talking about money. I'm talking about ideas that I'm seeing filtering up into the mainstream that used to be radical ideas, that we were talking about on blogs three or four years ago. So I'm starting to see the results of the conversation that we've been having for a long time filtering up into mainstream politics. I think that that's the major change.

It's obviously become more monetized, more professionalized, in many ways. You see the mainstream media moving online now in a big way. And, in the course of that, adopting many of the folk ways, attitudes, and styles that we invented. So the next challenge is to see whether or not the independent, political blogosphere will survive the professionalization of blogging.

I think it will, because you just can't stop it. It's like water. There'll always be room for independent voices that represent something that people aren't hearing or getting elsewhere. And the feedback aspect of it, the conversation that happens on independent blogs, is really different than it is on mainstream media sites. It's a very different and less serious political conversation that happens on those blogs than happens on ours.

We're in a big state of flux but, so far, I actually feel optimistic about the survival of the political blogosphere. I think the future looks pretty good. And I think a lot of it has to do with the liberal, political blogosphere. We're fairly serious people, serious about what we're doing. It's not a game, it's not a hobby. It's actually pretty real. And we're making headway. I'm kind of surprised by it. It just sort of happened. It evolved naturally.

18
Kevin Drum

Like some of the other bloggers profiled in this book, Kevin Drum is an accidental blogger. Having worked as Vice President of Marketing for Kofax Image Products, a software company, and, subsequently, as an independent consultant, he came across a number of political blogs and was so impressed by them that, within a couple of days, he decided to launch his own blog which he called *Calpundit* (Drum is originally from Orange County, California). His blog became so successful that only two years later, in 2004, he was invited by *Washington Monthly*, a progressive liberal magazine, to blog for them. Since 2008, his blog has been hosted by *Mother Jones*, another prominent liberal magazine.

While Drum, like some of his peers, came to blogging more or less by accident, he's set himself apart in the political blogosphere in several important ways. First, although Drum blogs for the liberal *Mother Jones*, he's widely known and respected for his non-dogmatic approach to blogging. In an increasingly polarized and tribal political blogosphere, where many liberal and conservative bloggers do little more than toe the party-line and only engage the other side to mock or attack, Drum strives to engage liberal and conservative thinking in genuine dialogue. He not only reads and cites various liberal and conservative bloggers on his site, but also questions political orthodoxies on either side. Moreover, Drum is widely known for his magazine-like, analytical approach to blogging. Instead of confining himself to short, narrative commentaries, his postings are relatively long and often feature original, statistical analyses as well as graphic displays of those analyses in the form of charts and figures. On a lighter note, Drum is also widely known as the originator of Friday catblogging whereby many bloggers draw back their claws a bit on Fridays and, in addition to their usual fare, also post pictures of their cats and other household pets.

#####

When did you take up blogging?

I took it up as a hobby back in the summer of 2002. I just opened up a *Blogspot* account and started doing it. I kept on doing it for about a year when, out of the blue, I got a call from the *Washington Monthly* asking me if I wanted to come to work for them full-time as a blogger. It was originally going to be just a temporary thing, for the 2004 presidential election. But when November rolled around, they were happy with the blog, and I was happy doing it. I was so happy about having a new career that I just kept on doing it. And I've been doing it ever since. So it was all completely accidental.

Was there anything in particular that attracted you to blogging?

I don't know how to say it but, for me, it was just a natural thing. I started reading blogs by accident. I don't even remember what the first one I read was. And two or three days later I started up a blog. It was just a medium that attracted me, the immediacy, the fact that there were lots of short takes on a lot of different issues rather than long takes on a few issues. I also liked the partisan nature of it, the personal nature of it, the first person nature of it. You had comments and would get a lot of interaction with readers. All of those things immediately attracted me to it.

I basically took to it like a duck to water. It's kind of funny but, if you go back and look at my earliest posts, they're not very different from the ones I write now. Hopefully, the ones I write now are a little bit better, but I don't think there's all that much of a difference.

What has kept you going all this time?

I was never a journalist before I did it. I was Vice President of Marketing for a software company. Like I said, I just took it up as a hobby; it just sort of happened. So it wasn't a matter of changing from one kind of journalism to another. And since I took it up as a hobby to begin with, I didn't really have any goals other than I enjoy writing about liberal politics.

**How does blogging, in your opinion, differ from
more conventional news analysis?**

Bloggers all interact with one another. And they interact very, very quickly whereas, say, newspaper columnists will write about the same issue and have different opinions but won't interact with each other directly or respond to each other's arguments. That only happens occasionally.

Where do you get your inspiration from?

I'm a man of habit, so I've got a bunch of blogs that I read regularly. There are 20 or 30 that I have on RSS feed and 30, 40, 50, perhaps 100 more, that I've bookmarked and read either daily or occasionally. I read all those blogs and probably a dozen traditional media sources like *The New York Times*, *The Washington Post*, the *Los Angeles Times*, and *The Wall Street Journal*.

I scan newspapers and I scan blogs every morning. Basically, I just look for stuff that I, for one reason or another, feel like I have something to say about. I write a post about it, and then I move on from there. It's not something I think about beforehand.

Does your reading also include conservative and libertarian blogs?

Yes, it does. My reading habits are certainly much more heavily weighted toward liberal blogs, but yes, I do read conservative and libertarian blogs.

Who do you have in mind when you blog?

I think of the audience mostly as liberal, political junkies. People who aren't really into politics aren't going to read this kind of stuff. I do policy blogging, and that means there are numbers and simple explanations. But these aren't white papers. It's not 10,000 words on a given topic.

What makes a lot of my stuff accessible to people, I think, is that they're interested in policy, but aren't going to read a long article. So, instead, I give it to them in 500 word chunks. Over the course of a year or two, they're going to get 10,000 words on the topic. They're just going to get it a few hundred words at a time.

Do you do anything in particular to attract and retain readers over time?

Not really. I just do what I do. I do, however, link to other bloggers a lot. If you want people to pay attention to you, you need to engage with the rest of the blogosphere.

More generally, I think that successful bloggers all appeal to a particular niche of readers. In my case it's mostly readers who're interested in a magazine-like, analytical approach. There are a lot of charts and figures and things like that that appeal to a certain kind of audience.

What, in your opinion, are the key features of a successful political blog?

It's hard to say because there are so many different kinds of blogs, so many ways to succeed. And they all succeed in different ways. The kind of blogging I do tends to be medium-length and fairly analytical, at least by blogging standards. That works well for me and other bloggers. But then you have guys like Atrios who succeeds because he's an uncanny ability to get at the heart of what liberals are thinking in just a few sentences. Then you've got guys like Glenn Greenwald, at the other end of the spectrum. He only posts once a day, and it's a long post. He's been immensely successful with that. You really have awfully successful blogs with quite different approaches. If five years ago you'd have asked me if someone like Glenn Greenwald could succeed, I'd said no. That's not what readers are looking for. And I'd have been wrong. That's exactly what some readers are looking for.

Either way, it's certainly both about quality and quantity. One thing that doesn't really get talked about a lot is that successful blogs almost always have a fair amount of quantity. Quality just isn't enough. The reason for that, I think, is that people get into the habit of reading a blog. This means that, unless you blog pretty frequently, people just don't get into the habit of checking your blog every day, or checking it two or three times a day, or putting it in their RSS feed. So you really need to have a fair amount of quantity. That's one of the reasons, I think, you've seen, especially over the past few years, a lot of growth in group blogs.

Going back to your own blog, why do you think you've been so successful?

Most blogs, on both the liberal and conservative side, tend to be very down the line, either liberal or conservative. They hardly ever question liberal or conservative policy except that, if you're liberal, you question it from the left and, if you're conservative, you question it from the right.

But very few bloggers question policy from the center. I do that because that's just how I feel. There are obviously people who're attracted to that kind of writing, people who at least occasionally question some of the orthodoxies from either side.

What advice would you give someone who wants to try to emulate your success?

My advice is to write about something that you're really interested in and that you really care about. The reason I say this is that blogging is very personal, very first person, very immediate. There's no editor in between you and the reader. So you get a sense of the person writing the blog. I feel like I can get a sense of whether they're writing something they really want to write about, or if they're just doing it because they feel obligated to do it, because this story is in the news today and they feel they ought to say something about it.

Do you have any other, more specific advice for aspiring political bloggers?

Sure. Don't think you can learn everything you need to learn just by reading blogs. You need to read books, too. A lot of bloggers think they can learn everything they need to learn from blogs or, at the most, from reading articles in *Slate, The New Republic* or whatnot. You really can't. If you really want to understand a few topics, you'll either need to read books on those topics, or at least read one or two books on a lot of topics, so you'll have a broad spectrum of knowledge.

One way or another, if you want to understand things, you've got to read books. It's the only thing that gives you the context to write intelligently about stuff.

Aside from that, don't try to be somebody else. If you try to copy them, you're going to fail. It's such a personal medium. It so much depends on writing in your own voice. It really has to be yours, not one you make up from somewhere else.

What are the most common mistakes that less experienced political bloggers tend to make?

One mistake is to think that they can do it, even if they don't really enjoy the pure writing aspect of it all that much. You have to enjoy writing. You really have to enjoy sitting down at a keyboard and typing words. If you don't, then you might as well just forget about it.

Another mistake is that new bloggers tend to blast out emails and market themselves immediately, like in their first week of blogging. That almost never works. Established bloggers know that lots of people get into blogging and don't stick with it. So they don't get a lot of attention, because we all know that anybody who's blasting out emails trying to promote themselves after a week's worth of blogging is probably not going to be around in the next few weeks.

So it's a waste of time. You need to do it for at least a few months. And, if you give up quickly because you don't have a big audience, that means you're not cut out for it in the first place.

When I started doing it, I'd an audience of 300 or 400 people after three months. That was all I could get right off the bat. Blogging has since become a big enough thing that people think they can get into it and immediately become the next Jane Hamsher.

It's not going to happen. You've got to be willing to stick to it for a while. And if you do try to market yourself, you need to be halfway intelligent about it. Don't start blasting out emails about your posts to your favorite bloggers every time you write something. You've got to figure out what different people are interested in and only market posts that you think they'd be interested in. And if you're going to do it, you need to engage with them on the blog. You need to engage with them, not through your publicity or marketing effort, but on the blog itself.

What trends do you see with respect to political blogging?

The biggest one is professionalization which comes in three ways. The first is from professionals who become bloggers like, say, Andrew Sullivan or Mickey Kaus, who were professional journalists before they started blogging. Number two would be people like me, who started as amateurs and then got hired by a magazine to write professionally. And, third, are people who stay independent, but become big enough that they can attract enough advertising and support from readers for it to become a full-time job. They become professionals in that it becomes a full-time job, and they get revenues from advertising and reader donations.

The professionalization of the political blogosphere has made a difference. There's a different tone now than when I first started blogging.

How has the tone changed?

When I started out, there was much more of a tendency to engage with the other side. Liberals and conservatives would attack each other, but we'd also engage with each other in at least a moderately serious way. Today, you get almost none of that. There's very little engagement between left and right. And what engagement there is tends to be pure attack. There's no real conversation at all. That's a difference that I think professionalization has brought about. The political blogosphere has become more tribal.

Whether you're liberal, conservative, or whatever, you belong to a particular tribe. And if you want to succeed, you really need to be part of that. You can't go outside the boundaries of the tribe as much as you could when I first started blogging.

Is that also how you earn your reputation in the political blogosphere?

Yes, because reputation in the political blogosphere is like reputation anywhere. What's important is reputation among your peers and, in the political blogosphere, your peers are other bloggers. Your peers aren't other newspaper columnists or television reporters. They are bloggers. And if you want traffic, if you want links, you've got to get it from other bloggers. You're not going to get that if you step too far off the reservation. So fewer and fewer bloggers do step off the reservation.

For that reason, like I said earlier, there's less serious engagement between left and right than there used to be. There's a lot of mockery and that's different from real conversation.

Aside from that, there are a lot more experts, whether from universities or from think-tanks, who blog today than when I started. And they are pretty good at it. Surprisingly good. Bloggers have a tendency to say they're not intimidated by experts, that you don't have to go along with what all the experts think. But they do. We all get intimidated by experts, because experts know a hell of a lot more than we do.

The fact that those experts are in the political blogosphere and engage with all the rest of us changes the way amateurs like me blog. It also changes the way outsiders view the political blogosphere. It's one thing when it's just somebody like me or Glenn Reynolds. It's another thing when it's Paul Krugman blogging. And it's a whole different thing when you've got prominent economists like Paul Krugman and Brad DeLong blogging. You have to take them seriously because these are the same people you'd be listening to if you were only reading newspapers or magazines.

19
Juan Cole

Among many other remarkable things, the emergence of the political blogosphere has helped amplify the popular reach and impact of academics. Previously sheltered within the proverbial ivory tower, talking primarily amongst themselves, now many academics have created political blogs where they bring their specialized knowledge to bear on a variety of political issues of concern to the wider public. Such is the case with Juan Cole, the author of one of the most respected foreign policy blogs, the liberal *Informed Comment*.

Although Cole, who holds a collegiate professorship in History at the University of Michigan, has been well-known in academic circles for decades, it wasn't until 2002, when he launched his blog, that he started to gain recognition as a leading public intellectual and an expert on the Middle East and South Asia. Since then, Cole has appeared on numerous television and radio shows both in the U.S. and abroad, written articles for some of the world's leading newspapers, including the *Guardian, Le Monde,* and the *Washington Post,* and testified before the U.S. Senate Committee on Foreign Relations. He's received many accolades for his blogging, including the prestigious "James Aronson Award for Social Justice Journalism" and two Koufax Awards — for "Best Expert Blog" and "Best Blog Post."

Cole, who lived and worked for almost a decade in the Middle East and South Asia, speaks and reads Arabic, Persian, and Urdu. He uses his extensive knowledge of those regions to comment on a broad range of foreign policy issues, including the U.S. invasions of Iraq and Afghanistan, the domestic politics of Iran and Pakistan, the emergence of Al-Qaeda and the Taliban, the Middle East Peace Process, and the War on Terror. His blog features commentary on articles in Western news media, summaries of articles from Middle Eastern news sources, including his own translations of Arabic and Farsi articles, as well as spirited discussions with both supporters and critics of his particular foreign policy views.

#####

What was the impetus for *Informed Comment*?

It was a direct result of the September 11 attacks. It so happened that my own personal, academic, and biographical trajectory overlapped a good deal with the terrain on which Al-Qaeda as an organization unfolded. I'd been in Egypt in the late 1970s when Ahmad al-Zawahiri emerged. I'd lived in Pakistan and had seen the Mujahedeen come to prominence.

As a result of my research in South Asia, I followed Pakistani politics all through the 1980s and 1990s. And you can't follow Pakistani politics without keeping one eye on Afghanistan. After September 11, there were a lot of questions in people's minds about what Al-Qaeda was, where it came from, what was going on in Afghanistan, and so forth.

I was on several email discussion lists back then and was able to answer some of the questions asked off the top of my head. I discovered that people wanted back-issues of those emails, but it's not convenient to dig back out an old email and send it off to someone.

From the very beginning, I was interested in the Internet as a communications tool. So I began my blog in the spring of 2002, initially as a way of having a place to publicly archive my email messages about Al-Qaeda and the War on Terror. That way, when someone asked me for a comment I'd made earlier on an email list, I could simply direct them to the blog so they could look it up themselves.

How has the experience been? Writing blog posts is obviously very different from more conventional academic writing.

When I was living in Beirut in the late 1970s, I'd a stint working for a newspaper as a translator. I also wrote a couple of original things. But it was mostly translating. So the habits of thought, the writing style and so forth that I developed when I was a journalist were very relevant to my blog.

I think one of the reasons why relatively few academics have made the transition to blogging is that they don't have that training in journalism. In fact, blogging transgresses most of the norms of academic writing. I remember one time I was on an email discussion list when a book by a friend of mine was critiqued. He emailed me, a little upset, saying: "I have to respond." And I said, "Well, I think you should." He said, "It'll just take me two weeks to get my material together." I responded, "Well, don't bother, then. Two weeks from now they won't remember. You'll just be reminding them that you'd been critiqued."

You shouldn't blog if you can't organize your thoughts quickly and write something clearly. You also have to be willing to let things go. You have to be willing for them not to be perfect. You have to be open to the possibility that they're mistaken.

Academic writing is all about forestalling those possibilities to the extent possible but at the cost of relevance. So we'll get excellent academic books about the war in Iraq after the U.S. archives for this period are opened in 2033.

What has kept you going all these years?

Initially, I suppose, it was the fact that the U.S. foreign policy establishment – the political and military establishment – was becoming profoundly involved in a region of the world that I knew well. Those projects that the U.S. government undertook generated large amounts of propaganda and a need for good information and analysis.

I felt a calling to address the public with the best information that I could gather, and the best analysis that I could perform, on these national projects. I also felt a duty to counter the propaganda. So it's basically a form of public truth-telling, which, I think, is one of the cornerstones of a democratic republic.

What role would you like *Informed Comment* to play in the political sphere more generally?

The goal of the blog is to serve as a classic liberal medium, in the sense that democracies thrive in the presence of a maximization of good information. I'm simply making information available to anyone who finds it valuable.

How do you decide what to blog about on any given day?

First of all I try to write blog entries on issues where I feel I can add value to the discussion. I check for what stories seem to be generating a certain amount of buzz. So I'll check *Technorati.com* and its most popular news and blog entries. I'll check *Google News*. I'll check various news aggregators that are driven by algorithms that express broad public interest in an issue. That'll tell me if there's anything out there that people are talking about and on which I might have a considered view and might be able to intervene in the conversation.

Who do you try to reach? Educated readers? Journalists? Policy-makers?

I try to reach them all. The public encompasses all of those people. And more. The Internet can break down barriers between social classes and persons of various educational attainments. I get sharp comments back from workers, people in retail sales – all kinds of people interested in what the U.S. government is doing abroad. I like that democratic character of the medium.

I do know that journalists and policy-makers read it. I don't typically, when I sit down and write a blog entry, have an image of who I'm writing for. It's much more general than that. And I'm gratified if others, including colleagues and other professionals, find it useful. But it's written for a broad audience.

Aside from what you've mentioned already, do you do anything else to attract and retain readers?

Regularity is very important. Early in my blogging days, I experimented with not blogging on weekends, and I know some bloggers who don't. I'd go on vacation for three weeks and put up a sign saying, "Gone Fishing." I discovered through the blog metrics that there was a very substantial decline in readership when I did that. So I concluded that a daily entry, however short, was important to keeping people coming back.

And then, like I said earlier, I'm kind of like a spider on a web, trying to keep a sense of what people are interested in. Attention has shifted from Al-Qaeda to Iraq, and I've made that shift. It's not that I've stopped blogging about Al-Qaeda, but I blog more about Iraq now. Now, I'm sensing a tremendous shift of interest away from Iraq and toward Iran.

Again, it's not that I've stopped following Iraq. But I admit to following the crowd in that regard. That's to say, I view the blog as a place where I can intervene in whatever the day's debates are. And, if the debate changes, I'll follow it. So I shifted to blogging about Iran a lot. And, in fact, my traffic is larger than it's ever been. The Iran story has generated enormous interest, and I've the credentials as an Iranist.

What, in your opinion, are the most salient features of a high-quality political blog? And which political blogs do you find best embody those features?

I think there are a number of features. One is expertise. The really good political blogs are written by people who've some area of expertise that they can bring to bear on the discussion.

Take, for instance, *Talking Points Memo*. Joshua Marshall has a Ph.D. in American History, and he's decided to cover Congress. He brings to that task not just journalistic skills and being in Washington, D.C. but also a broad understanding of the history of American politics.

I'm not saying that you have to have a Ph.D. to be a good blogger, but I'm saying that expertise is important. Sometimes the expertise can be indirect. Take, for instance, Steve Clemons from *The Washington Note*. Here's somebody who's an expert on Japanese politics. He doesn't talk very often about Japanese politics on his blog. He talks about Washington politics. But when he discusses Washington politics or international affairs, as he often does, his background as an expert on Japanese politics does him good.

So the expertise might be direct, or it might be indirect. But it's there. There are certainly generalists who are good political bloggers. But having expertise is an advantage in and of itself.

Blogging, in my view, is a form of journalism. So a nose for stories is also very important. Take, for instance, someone like Jane Hamsher at *Firedoglake*. She could see the significance of the Scooter Libby/Valerie Plame story and the subsequent trial. She went and sat in the courtroom every day, along with other bloggers at *Firedoglake* like Marcy Wheeler. There are lots and lots of journalists in Washington, D.C. but nobody else went and sat in the courtroom every day. Jane had a nose for that story, and she followed it intensively. That really put Jane and her blog on the map. So you could have a lot of expertise but still be tone deaf to stories, and you wouldn't be able to generate hits.

Aside from expertise and a nose for stories, a good political blogger also needs a strong point of view and be able to show attitude. This is an aspect of blogging that's common to opinion pages in newspapers but which, I think, is disturbing to academics. Academic discourse is about wringing out personal opinion and attitude, but it produces bland writing.

This may not be the first thing people think about but, just as a good novelist is a good novelist in part because he or she has developed a distinctive voice, so a good political blogger has a voice. It's the voice that, at least in part, sells the blog.

On that note, what do you do to "sell" your blog?

I try to follow stories of broad, popular interest to which I can contribute something, regardless of whether it's analysis of evidence or original newsgathering, of which I do some. With regard to the war in Iraq and, of course, Al-Qaeda, my ability to read Arabic is important.

I've also done research in Pakistan, and I know Persian and Urdu. So Iran and Afghanistan are countries I've written about professionally as well. It so happens that that has been the terrain of American foreign policy over the last ten years.

I try to bring to bear readings and paraphrases from the indigenous press. This is something the Internet has made possible, because most newspapers in the Middle East now have an online edition. I can begin to read the next day's newspapers from the region at 10 or 11pm, and I can begin to think about it.

So one thing I bring to the table is linguistic competence and access to online newspapers, speeches and reports. Another thing I bring to bear is social science judgment as a social historian. I find that analysts who don't know a region well, or only know it from a particular angle, often get the proportions wrong. When the press reports on a bombing in a city, the journalists often don't tell you how big or important the city is, who lives there, etc. I contextualize.

One of the things that I've had to offer people, and which has been appreciated by my audience, has been a firm sense of what I'd call proportionality. I've written that, when the Bush administration went into Iraq, it was underestimating Arab nationalism. The idea that the Iraqis would be grateful to have a foreign military in their midst struck me as ridiculous.

With regard to more recent events, the Obama administration was saying that Pakistan was six months away from collapse. On an episode of Bill Moyers's *Journal*, I tried to poke holes in that. So it's not just linguistic competence. It's also a lifetime of social science analysis of the region.

Why do you think *Informed Comment* has been so successful?

I can tell you exactly why. The aftermath of September 11 – the War on Terror and then the Iraq and Afghanistan wars – was a right-wing narrative. They benefited the right-wing in the U.S. politically. The American left, at the time, was in some disarray. They were blindsided by Al Gore's defeat, and they were extremely puzzled, I think, when they lost again in 2004. They were getting beaten up on pretty badly. It was difficult for the left to respond to the Bush administration's triumphalist narratives about the onward march of democracy in the region.

I was blogging about the Middle East and South Asia from a left-of-center point of view. And I brought not only a left-of-center analysis but also good credentials. I was a professor at the University of Michigan. I was respected.

Everybody on the left felt that they ought to recommend a site dealing with those foreign policy issues, the War on Terror, the war in Iraq. I was just about it for the left at that time, so I was added to an enormous numbers of blog rolls and then the number just kept proliferating. I also think it gave the American left more confidence in developing a critique of the Bush administration's foreign policy to have someone like me on their side

Since I present solid information and analysis, a lot of right-wing and right-of-center bloggers also added me to their blog rolls. They were more interested in nuggets of information than my points of view, however.

What advice do you have for people who want to launch a political blog themselves?

If you want to start a successful blog, and you're really dedicated to the idea of doing it, you should just do it and do it regularly. Set standards for yourself and meet them regularly. Don't worry about traffic.

In fact, the first year that I blogged, my traffic was almost non-existent. Sometimes, I'd get 25 hits a day. I'd give a talk some place, mention that I had a blog, and it'd go up to 120. Later in my career I'd get 40,000-50,000 daily hits.

There's no gaming the system. The Internet is a distributed information system. It's really like the old adage that, if you make a better mousetrap, the world will beat a path to your door. So, if you do quality blogging on a daily basis, over time people will link to you and you'll be found. If you're offering something the public wants, then they'll find you.

The other wrinkle, however, is that when I started out, the political blogosphere was the Wild Frontier and very individualistic. Things have shifted. So I'd tell the person to consider getting a slot at *The Huffington Post*. Arianna Huffington has two kinds of people at *The Huffington Post*. She's a journalistic staff, but she'll often give op-ed writers a perch.

Blogging at *The Huffington Post* or other "umbrella" sites has certain advantages. If you did something the editors liked enough to put on the front-page, that would make you in and of itself because you'd get 50,000 hits.

Are there certain mistakes that less experienced political bloggers should be especially mindful of?

Yes. Political blogging is a lot like journalism. So going off half-cocked, single sourcing, making all the same mistakes that journalists sometimes make is a problem. It's important that bloggers be careful about sources because a lot of blogging, of course, is parasitical of what journalists are doing.

Political bloggers would do themselves a favor by doing some reading in journalistic standards before they start out. Learn how to deal with sources, how to contextualize, and how to resist the temptation to punditry. Don't just shoot off an opinion about something that you don't really know that much about because that's dangerous.

If you make a significant error by depending on a single source, or shoot off your mouth about something, you can get burned as unreliable. So, sure, mistakes can be costly.

Briefly put, what trends do you see with respects to the future of political blogging?

One of the biggest trends is conglomeration. A lot of corporate media have made a place for bloggers. There are obviously efficiencies associated with conglomeration, but the trend worries me. People do get fired because of their point of view, as with Dan Froomkin at *The Washington Post*'s blog.

When I started out, nobody would get fired. In fact, it'd have been ridiculous to talk about a blogger being fired. It disturbs me that you're at a point where a neo-conservative editorial board can make or break bloggers. So the downside to conglomeration may be some loss of individual autonomy.

20
Cheryl Contee

In many people's minds, the political blogosphere is composed of two easily defined and opposing camps: liberal and conservative/libertarian blogs. But, especially during the past five years, thousands of blogs have appeared which, in addition to their political orientation, also define themselves by their ethnic affiliation, notably African-American, Asian, and Hispanic blogs. Among the numerous African-American blogs, the most widely read is the liberal *Jack & Jill Politics*, written by Cheryl Contee, her co-blogger Baratunde Thurston, as well as half a dozen part-time contributors.

Contee's goals for *Jack & Jill Politics*, which she launched in 2006, is to provide a space for the expression and discussion of African-American, middle-class perspectives on politics, to challenge the misconception that a few, well-known public figures, such as Jesse Jackson and Al Sharpton, are representative of the diversity of perspectives among African-Americans, and, most generally, to correct faulty mainstream news media portrayals of African-Americans. As one of the first political blogs – African-American or otherwise – that came out in support of Barack Obama's run for president, *Jack & Jill Politics* also has become a site to which people of all ethnicities and walks of life go for a strong, African-American perspective on the governance of the first black President of the U.S.

The rapid growth of *Jack & Jill Politics* is attributable to several factors, including the fact that Contee and Thurston very early on reached out to other African-American political bloggers and received support from larger, more established liberal bloggers like Jane Hamsher of *Firedoglake*. *Jack & Jill Politics* has become so well-known and respected that it's now on the White House's official media list.

Aside from running *Jack & Jill Politics*, Contee is a Partner at Fission Strategy, a consulting firm that helps non-profit organizations and foundations use social media to champion their causes, and has more than a decade of executive experience with interactive media campaigns. Prior to joining Fission Strategy, she was Vice President and Lead Digital Strategist for the public relations firm Fleishman-Hillard's West Coast region, Vice

President for Issue Dynamics Inc, a smaller, Washington, D.C.-based public relations firm, Web Director for Oceana, an international marine conservation organization, and directed web site production and strategic communications at a number of organizations, including the Business Software Alliance, Discovery Communications, and the U.S. Institute of Peace. She graduated from Yale University and has an International Executive MBA from Georgetown University.

Contee has received numerous accolades over the years for her blogging and interactive media campaigns. Named one of the "Most Influential Women in Technology" by the magazine *Fast Company*, she's included in the online magazine *The Root*'s list of 100 established and emerging African-American leaders, and sits on various blogging boards and advisory committees, including *Blogging While Brown, BlogHer, and Netroots Nation.*

What made you decide to launch *Jack & Jill Politics*?

I started *Jack & Jill Politics* in July of 2006. It was actually an idea that was presented to me by a friend who was already a blogger. He'd noticed that there weren't enough black, political bloggers, especially heterosexual, black, political bloggers.

So I launched the blog and, after a couple of months, it became clear to me that not only did we need more content but, more importantly, that we needed a black male voice on the blog. While black men and black women have a lot in common, we also sometimes see things differently or just comment from a different perspective. So I invited Baratunde Thurston to join me.

How has the experience been so far?

It's been like riding a rocket. It was a surprise that the blog grew so quickly, that we really had identified a need in the marketplace, and that people responded.

We got some initial support from larger, progressive bloggers like Markos Moulitsas at *Daily Kos* and Jane Hamsher at *Firedoglake*, as well as other big bloggers. That was really helpful in terms of generating traffic and making allies. And, as the black, political blogosphere itself started to grow, we also got a lot of links and attention from those blogs.

We joined the Afrosphere which is a network of mostly politically-oriented, black bloggers. We also made sure to link to other politically-oriented black blogs, as well as to cultural black blogs, and Asian blogs like *AngryAsianMan*. So we really try to represent a spectrum while retaining our focus on the African-American community.

**Why did you decide to call the blog *Jack & Jill Politics* instead of
using your real names? You're obviously not
trying to hide your identities.**

Actually, when we first launched the blog, Baratunde and I were
anonymous. We'd very different careers, and what we were doing was very
new and innovative.

There was no model for what we were doing. So we weren't really sure
how it'd be received, and whether it'd have an impact. But we knew that it
was important to speak out, represent, and create a community of African-
Americans who were passionate; to sort of push back on media perceptions
of how we think and how we feel about certain issues.

One of our campaigns in the beginning was to push back on the notion
that Al Sharpton and Jesse Jackson speak for black America. We were very
clear that, in fact, they're often ridiculed and lampooned, and that there are
lots and lots of other spokespeople out there.

On that note, what are your goals for the site?

When we first launched the blog, there weren't as many African-
American, political blogs. Now there are literally thousands. So part of it
was just to add other perspectives to the progressive political blogosphere.

We also felt, at the time, that it was difficult to get the perspective of
the African-American middle-class, especially with respect to politics and
culture. Even though the majority of African-Americans are middle class,
we're not visible on TV or even in many newspapers.

It was also a very conscious way of saying, "Look, we represent normal,
black people who're sitting next to you in your office or in the cubicle next
to you."

Also, at the time we launched the blog, Dave Chappelle had exited the
scene in a very public way. Chris Rock's career had its ups and downs. We
saw that there was an opening for some satire, the type of black political
satire that's very popular and well-received.

**What role do you see *Jack & Jill Politics* playing
in the political sphere more generally?**

Our role has changed over time. We used to be very much the underdog
and needed a lot of help. But that changed with the Obama campaign,
because we were one of the first blogs that had a significant audience
supportive of Obama. Obama campaign operates have said to me, "You
guys were really among the first that were behind us."

The fact that we were a clearinghouse for African-Americans made us a very strong site where people supporting Barack Obama could come. We'd a pretty strong community before that, but that really took the site to a whole new level. Especially when Obama became the nominee, people of all walks of life and all ethnicities were looking for a strong, black perspective on a black, political candidate.

Those are different roles that we've played. After the election, we asked ourselves whether there was still a place for *Jack & Jill Politics*, and what we should do. It became clear to us that, even though the majority of Americans voted for Obama, there are still a lot of people who didn't vote for him. And there's still a lot of hatred, a lot of fear, out there. There are voices, particularly on the right, that are saying things that are at best racist, at worst dangerous. Dangerous and unpatriotic. We continue to push back on the media when they portray African-American perspectives and our experiences inaccurately.

African-Americans don't just care about urban issues. We're a very engaged culture politically. At many African-American kitchen tables you've got spirited discussions about things like health care, the economy, and the environment. So we feel our role hasn't changed as much as we thought it would, except that it started in opposition to the standing government and their treatment of African-Americans. Now we are supportive while focused on accountability.

Where do you get your inspiration from?

I'd say that inspiration comes from a number of sources that have changed over time. Now we receive press releases from the White House. We're on their media list, which is not something I'd ever imagined. It's just incredible.

I also get a lot of inspiration from the blog itself. Our community identifies stories that we then elevate. I'm on various listservs of bloggers where we talk amongst ourselves, and they often have very good ideas. Readers email me, too.

We're also, of course, responsive to the issues of the day. I read newspapers online, and I watch *CNN* and *MSNBC*, even *Fox News*. I watch all of those, and I respond to them, too.

Who are you trying to reach?

Our goal is to reach a lot of different audiences at the same time. I'd say that our primary audiences are policy-makers and journalists. Those are the people who can ultimately make the changes that we want made. But, of course, also the community itself. Without our community our voice doesn't make a difference. What makes a difference is when we write something and see that there are 150 or 300 comments.

Do you do anything in particular to make the blog as attractive to readers as possible?

We do a few things. The open thread was something we started during the presidential election. We found that we were getting so many comments on so many topics that we wanted to encourage that.

We also comment on the comments, so that people can see that we're reading and listening. I don't personally get to every post, but I make it a habit to go back and at least read what people have said and respond, either in the comments or in a follow-up post. Those are some of the strategies that we employ.

What, in your opinion, are the defining features of a high-quality political blog?

That it's updated frequently and responsive to the issues of the day. Strong writing. I don't think we'd have been as successful if people didn't relate on some level to the way we write. We try to be funny as well as serious. So part of it is tone and personality, a really strong tone and personality. Even though we have readers from all walks of life, we're very focused on speaking to a particular community. Other readers, I think, like to lurk or eavesdrop. They want to know what that community is thinking.

On that note, what do you do to promote your blog?

In the beginning we did a lot of emailing on listservs, and we still do that. We send our stories to other bloggers, though we haven't done much of that lately because we haven't had to. People read what we write.

Our promotional strategy hasn't changed that much. What's new and different is that we've been inviting other people to blog for us. For example, Ben Jones, who is now at the White House, has blogged on our site.

Do you use *Facebook, Twitter* or other means to promote your blog?

Sure. We've a *Facebook* page and a *Twitter* auto-feed to feed our blog posts to our audience. Both of those have grown pretty quickly. So we're doing a lot to reach out to our readers. The idea is not only to bring emerging, black leaders to *Jack & Jill Politics*, but also to promote those folks. We're reaching out to our readers off the blog to experience our content.

What do you think has been the key to your success?

I think it really comes back to good writing. I think it's good writing, and the fact that we were in the right place at the right time. There was a real hole in the political discourse, and there were real problems with how African-Americans felt they were perceived by the media. So I think it was really strong content plus meeting a need that was unmet.

**What advice do you have for someone who
wants to try to emulate your success?**

I'd tell the person not to just start blogging. First get to know the community that you're seeking to enter. That way you can get a sense of who the leaders are and where your blog might fit in. It's important to consider where there's potentially a space that's not being filled, that is, a voice that's not being heard, a topic that's not being addressed very well. All that's really critical.

I also think it's important to link to those other blogs. No one is that interested in a blog that isn't clearly a part of a community, and being part of a community means linking to - dialoging with - other bloggers. Try to figure out if there are relevant listservs, or if you can use *Twitter* to engage other bloggers and your audience. And make sure that you've got an RSS feed that's operational.

**What is the biggest mistake that less experienced
political bloggers tend to make?**

The biggest mistake that I see is a failure to show a strong voice and personality. That's a really big problem. It's not that interesting to people if you're just publishing your press releases or e-newsletters. This doesn't mean that you can't take some of the content from your press releases or e-newsletter and use it in your blog. But having that real, personal voice is critical.

Another mistake is failing to read other blogs because reading is critical. Yet another mistake, which I see all the time, is the failure to use a popular, standard blogging platform. A lot of people try to bootstrap or create these faux blogs, but it just doesn't work. There are blogging tools out there, and you should use those. There's a reason people use them.

Briefly put, how do you feel the political blogosphere has evolved over time?

I'd say that, from a macro perspective, we've gone from being seen as crackpots to becoming mainstream, important voices. Voices that are legitimate, yet different from mainstream media. The organizations that interact with the political blogosphere see us as allies, even though they may not see us as journalists. I don't consider myself a journalist. I consider myself more of a community leader.

Where do you see political blogging heading?

As to the future, I think that blogging will become even more sophisticated. It's already sophisticated but will become more sophisticated in terms of how to generate advertising revenues, creating viable business models, and how bloggers work together. Because there are more blogs and growing audiences, I think blogging will not only become more sophisticated but also more powerful.

Conclusion:
How to Plan, Produce, and Promote a Successful Political Blog

During my conversations with 20 of the world's top political bloggers, these individuals talked at length about what others should and shouldn't do if they want to make it in the political blogosphere. Taken together, their advice amounts to a comprehensive blueprint on how to *plan*, *produce*, and *promote* a highly successful political blog.

Planning

> I know that a lot of people will read a couple of blogs and decide that it looks easy. But it's not easy. So it's really worth thinking about it. What could I do? What level of interest do I have in this? How committed am I? What is it that I'm bringing to the table? (Matthew Yglesias.)

It might be tempting, especially if you've never blogged before, to go to one of the many free blogging platforms, set up a blog in no time, and then start blogging about whatever political topics happen to be in the news. That would be a mistake, however. Political blogging may look easy but does in fact require a lot of careful planning if you're to succeed at it.

The first question you ought to ask yourself is whether you've a genuine passion for blogging. "The key to any successful blog," says Taegan Goddard, "is that the person running it has a complete passion for it." It's important to be passionate about blogging for several reasons. Most obviously, if you're genuinely passionate, you're likely to stay with it and patiently work to increase your readership over time. If not, you'll quickly get bored, and so will your dwindling number of readers. There's another, more specific reason why passion is such an important precondition for success. If you're passionate, your personality will come through in your blogging, and readers will end up trusting you. Unlike traditional news organizations, where readers' trust lies with the underlying institution (say, the *New York Times*) more so than with the individual journalist, blog readers' trust rests solely with the person writing the blog. The passion you feel shouldn't just be about the political topics you blog about; it should encompass the writing process itself. Kevin Drum puts it well: "You have to enjoy writing. You really have to enjoy sitting down at a keyboard and typing words. If you don't, then you might as well just forget about it."

Assuming that you're indeed passionate about blogging, the next step is to decide on a particular niche, and a particular focus. If you're to achieve success as a political blogger, you need to find a topic that'll allow you to stand out in the political blogosphere. Jane Hamsher says: "You have to do something special. You have to do something unique. You have to find a niche and fill it," or, as Andrew Malcolm puts it, "your blog needs to do something that other people's blogs don't do." According to John Hawkins, "all the best of the best have something unique about them. You can always go out, if you think about it enough, and find something that the best blogs do better than anybody else. Every one of them, if you go down the list and break it down, has something unique that they do."

A common mistake that new political bloggers make is to try to establish themselves as generalists or, as Arianna Huffington puts it, "to try to be all things at once." While some of the largest and most successful political blogs, including Huffington's own blog, are indeed generalist, these have been in existence for years and have resources at their disposal that aren't readily available to the newly-established blogger. Even these blogs have certain topics or "fields of strength," as Tyler Cowen calls it, which anchor everything else that they do.

Regardless of which particular niche you decide to fill, it's essential that you're genuinely interested in it and knowledgeable about it. Since blogging is such a personal medium, your readers will immediately sense whether you're blogging about something because you truly care about it, or whether you're doing it because the topic is in the news and you feel obligated to say something about it. You also need to know a lot about the topic of your blogging. Many people have strong opinions about a variety of political topics, but few have any specialized knowledge. As Ben Smith puts it, "I don't particularly care about your opinion of President Obama. Why should I? But if you know something about U.S.–Canada relations, I'd tell you to start a blog about that. Maybe I can learn something from it." More generally, says Smith, "There's a real hunger and demand for information, but there's a glut of opinions." So having that specialized knowledge will help you stand out in the political blogosphere.

Thus, as you plan your blog, you need to ask yourself why other people would be reading it. What is it you know that other political bloggers don't know or don't know as well? This is especially important, Matthew Yglesias stresses, "if you're new and don't have an institution backing you. People are instinctively going to be a little bit wary. So you really have to find subjects you're knowledgeable about, and deliver information that, if other people link to you, they don't wind up looking like idiots." Being knowledgeable about a given topic doesn't merely entail being at the forefront of current debates in the political blogosphere. You also need to read books about your topic. "One way or another," says Kevin Drum, "if you want to understand things, you've got to read books. It's the only thing that gives you the context to write intelligently about stuff."

John Hawkins sums up this line of advice well:

> Choose a topic that you're interested in, that you can write a lot about, and that you can be better at than everybody else. Don't try to compete with 5,000 other bloggers who're already running similar sites.

One profitable niche, if you don't already have one in mind, would be to focus on the area where you live and the particular, political issues facing it. A lot of people want to blog about the big national and international issues. Many will find that it's a crowded space in which it's hard to break through, whereas someone who has a passion for blogging about their city or town will find that they may not have much competition, but that people still care about what happens locally. The rapid decline of local and regional news media, especially newspapers, across the U.S. has left an information gap that's waiting to be filled by political bloggers. As Matthew Yglesias puts it, "If someone wrote a really good news and public affairs blog about the greater Detroit area, the fact that that metro region now has a newspaper which doesn't even publish seven days a week would draw a lot of readers to it. And it becomes pretty obvious what value you might add relative to other people. You know what happened at the City Council meeting."

Once you've decided on your niche, you'll need to do some research to better understand the larger universe of blogs of which your particular blog would be a part. You should, as Cheryl Contee puts it, "get to know the community that you're seeking to enter." Understanding the larger blogging community — i.e. what other political bloggers are doing and not doing in your particular area — will not only help you determine where your blog is best situated; it'll also help you identity other bloggers who might be willing to promote your blog. Unfortunately, many new political bloggers fail to do the necessary research, and, as a result, end up appearing less than impressive in the eyes of the very bloggers on which their success depends. "There's this presumption," says Nick Gillespie, "that the world was born when you were born, a lack of interest in the past and what has already been done. I find that off-putting."

Before you're ready to start blogging, there are a couple of important decisions to make, namely whether to start out on your own or to do so together with one or more like-minded people, and whether to use one of the many popular blogging platforms or to create your own domain name. If you've a lot of time at your disposal — and political blogging is indeed time-consuming if it's to be done well — a solo blog could be the right option for you. However, it may be advisable to join forces with one or more people, who, you believe, would complement your particular strengths. Even if you've all the time in the world, there's obviously strength in numbers. By creating a group blog rather than an individual blog, says Matthew Yglesias, "you'll get more content up. You'll have more ability to do outreach to people and just more ability to deliver consistency and build an audience over time."

Regardless of how you decide to proceed, it's advisable to follow what Eric Olsen calls a "dual approach" to blogging: start your own blog while simultaneously contributing to one or more of the larger group blogs. That way, you'll be able to make contact with some of the more established political bloggers and, equally importantly, alert readers to the existence of your own blog. As Nick Gillespie puts it, "It's important to have as many contact points as possible with the audiences, with the communities that you want to be part of."

While it's useful, especially when you're first starting out, to contribute to several of the larger group blogs, you may want to narrow that number down over time so that you won't spread yourself too thin. You don't want to make the decision about which group blogs to contribute to solely on the basis of their readership figures. Rather, Eric Olsen says, you should make your decision based on "where you feel most comfortable, where you feel most challenged, where you feel you're reaching people who're important to you for whatever reason."

Finally, you need to decide whether to go with one of the pre-existing blogging platforms or whether to create your own domain name— both options have their advantages and disadvantages. Popular blogging platforms like *Blogger*, *Typepad*, and *WordPress* are easy to navigate, and you can be up and running in no time. A drawback, however, is that using one of these platforms can make you appear less serious than if you had your own domain name. "A lot of people, particularly the more sophisticated bloggers out there," says Taegan Goddard, "won't take you as seriously as if you had your own domain name." This is significant, considering that these are the very people you need to help you promote your blog. While hosting your own domain will certainly make your blog appear more serious and professional, setting it up and running it might require help from someone with expertise in website development and design. This is an expense that you might feel more comfortable incurring once you've been blogging for a while and have decided that political blogging is indeed your true passion.

Producing

> Many people write material in order to demonstrate how much they know, or to put forth a point of view they feel strongly about. But they sometimes forget who the reader is, and what the reader needs to know.... So the one piece of advice I'd give people is to look at their material through the eyes of the reader who doesn't know you, who doesn't care who you are, and who needs to be given a reason to read the next sentence of your posting and continue all the way through." (Thomas Lifson.)

Once the preparatory work is completed, you're ready to start producing your blog. There are a number of things you can do to make your blog as attractive as possible. The most important thing upon which everything else depends is putting your readers first and considering what they'd like to know. While it's essential that you select a topic you know a lot about, you won't be successful unless you find a way to convey that knowledge in a manner that's truly compelling to your readers. As Andrew Malcolm puts it,

> You've got to make people want to read it. It's a choice after all. It's like that old story about the Hollywood mogul who made all these successful movies in the 1930s and then had a bust. He said, 'If they don't want to come, you can't stop them.' It's true. You have to make people want to come. They're not going to habitually come over to your place, if they're going to get bored three times a day. Just as they're not going to buy a newspaper or a magazine that tells them what they already know or says it in a boring way.

Indeed, if readers aren't interested by the first paragraph, whatever you say in subsequent paragraphs is irrelevant because they'll leave.

One way to keep readers engaged is to use what Andrew Malcolm calls his "lingerie" approach to blogging, or the principle that "it's what you can't see that interests you, that appeals to you." Instead of giving away the whole picture at once, it may be useful to slowly reveal where you're heading. "The subtle result," as Malcolm puts it, "is that you're drawn into to wonder what it is, to continue to look and see more."

There are as many approaches to political blogging as there are political bloggers out there, so you need to find the one most suitable to your particular topic and temperament. Be yourself, and do only what comes naturally to you. "Trying to be someone else, trying to take on a different voice," says Taegan Goddard, "never works." Kevin Drum agrees, arguing that you should never "try to be somebody else. If you try to copy them, you're going to fail. It's such a personal medium. It so much depends on writing in your own voice. It really has to be you, not one you make up from somewhere else." Never compromise your integrity by pandering to readers, but tell the truth as you see it. Political blogging, as Thomas Lifson puts it, is "about not omitting the facts that are inconvenient to the analysis."

It's also essential that you update your blog frequently with new and original content. Political blog readers behave much like traditional newspaper readers in that, over time, they develop a habit of reading certain blogs and come to expect that these are continuously updated. "Successful blogs," says Kevin Drum, "almost always have a fair amount of quantity. Quality just isn't enough. The reason for that, I think, is that people get into a habit of reading a blog. This means that, unless you blog pretty frequently, people just don't get into the habit of checking your blog every day." "The idea," as Matthew Yglesias puts it, "is to discourage people from drifting away. If you give them a break, they might find that there's something else that's just as good, and they might go away."

You should update your blog at least daily. "When somebody comes over to your blog," John Hawkins stresses, "you don't want them to come over and say, 'Okay, they did a post last Tuesday, and there's one from this Friday.' If you want to be a successful blogger, you've got to do a large amount of work. You've got to do a consistent amount of work. If you're not doing that, you're not going to be successful." Taegan Goddard agrees, arguing that "if you want to build a readership, it has to be a daily thing." If possible, you may want to update your blog several times a day. As Rogers Cadenhead puts it: "The people who keep making you come back to the trough all day are going to be the most successful." But you don't want to blog so frequently that the quality of your postings suffer. According to Steve Clemons, a common misconception among new political bloggers is that "they have to be out there all the time, so they quickly outrun their span of knowledge. They read something quickly, think they know it, and end up creating a small disaster. That undermines their credibility and makes them look trivial." More generally, says Juan Cole, "don't just shoot off an opinion about something that you don't know that much about." If you do, "you can get burned as unreliable."

Your blog shouldn't just be updated at least daily; it should consistently feature new and original content. "If you want to be taken seriously," says Jim Hoft, "you have to have continuously new material." Arianna Huffington agrees, arguing that "it's essential, online, that you have fresh content. Otherwise, people will stop coming." New political bloggers, unfortunately, often fail to heed that advice and instead merely echo what more prominent bloggers have already said. "New bloggers," in John Hawkins' experience, "will often take the latest story on the *Drudge Report*, write up a post about it, perhaps 50 words, and then they'll send me a link to the story and their brief comment. I ask myself, 'Why?' There are 500 people writing about that already." Or, as Ben Smith puts it, "The most boring thing in the world is to read at 4pm whatever talking points the Democratic and Republication National Committees put out at 10 am and have already been filtered through the blogs; to get the second and third ripple of what has already happened."

More generally, a common mistake new political bloggers make is to try to recreate an established blog. Says Heather Parton: "They're basically replicating what they've seen as being successful. The problem is that there are so many blogs that those formulas don't work with a new blog. You have to invent a new kind of blog in order to be successful, and people do that."

Political blogging isn't just about you; it's equally about your relationship with your readers and their relationships with one another. It's about the creation of community. In much the same way that your blog needs to be clearly situated within a larger community of like-minded blogs, you need to find ways to make your blog a community unto itself. Nick Gillespie puts it well when he says that a strong sense of community "is absolutely key to any successful blog where you're creating, either been the writers and the readers, or among both, some sense that we're all in the same room. You need to cultivate a sense that this is a place you can go to, to both learn something new and different and be challenged, but also to be accepted and feel a fraternal sense of dialogue."

There are many ways in which you can create that sense of community on your blog. You can offer your readers opportunities to interact with you and with one another, such as by allowing reader comments to your postings, having open threads in which your readers can decide on their own sub-topics and discuss them with each other, and even offering your most frequent and valuable commenters diaries through which they can contribute to your blog on a more regular and independent basis. If your blog isn't only devoted to a particular topic but to a specific political course, you can interview prominent politicians or allow them to guest-blog and then invite reactions from your readers, solicit campaign contributions and otherwise mobilize around the cause, and post information about upcoming political rallies and votes. Indeed, your interactions with readers shouldn't be confined to the blog itself. If you want to create a strong sense of community, says Lew Rockwell, "you also have to be welcoming to your readers and always reply to them when they write to you. You have to do so politely, even if they're very critical of you."

Soliciting reader input will not only help you create a strong sense of community; it's also likely to supply you with all kinds of material for your own postings that you may not even have considered. Reader input can, as Rogers Cadenhead puts it, "be a real godsend for coming up with interesting content." More generally, listening attentively to what your readers have to say will give you a better sense of what's important to them. During my conversation with Cadenhead, he mentioned the so-called "Kelo Decision," a U.S. Supreme Court ruling which, in Cadenhead's own estimation, wasn't that significant but, as it turned out, inspired much heated debate among his readers. As Cadenhead said, "I've to admit that had it been solely up to me, it wouldn't have gotten as much play, because I just didn't see it as being as important as did the users."

Being a member of that larger community of listeners and learners also means that you should approach your blogging with a certain degree of humility and not assume the stance of an all-knowing authority whose only responsibility is to teach your readers the correct way of looking at things. "As a contributor," Nick Gillespie admits," I've expertise in certain areas, and I can speak with authority on those areas. In other areas I'll cede the fact that my authority is limited. So your audience needs respect in two ways. One is to give them information that's reliable, useful, and interesting. But the audience also deserves respect in terms of you acknowledging the limits of your understanding." You're bound to make mistakes on a regular basis, even if you only blog about your particular area of expertise. "If you blog every day, or even every week," says Tyler Cowen, "you're going to say a lot of stuff. A lot of it will be either wrong or just not exactly the way you wanted it to be. If you don't admit that to yourself, you're fooling yourself." According to Cowen, there are several ways you can respond to that: "One is despair. You can quit blogging. The other is not just to try to be more correct the next time around, but to try to teach your readers how you're learning from your mistakes so they can learn that same skill."

More generally, bloggers must accept the fact that they relinquish control once they've posted something. Political blogging, according to Eric Olsen, "is like having a child. Once you send that story into the world, once that story is published, you don't control it anymore. It becomes the purview of the readers and the commenters." Indeed, trying to exert control would, Olsen says, "take the heart and soul out of it."

Promoting

> Reputation in the political blogosphere is like reputation anywhere. What's important is reputation among your peers and, in the political blogosphere, your peers are other bloggers. Your peers aren't other newspaper columnists or television reporters. They are bloggers. And if you want traffic, if you want links, you've got to get it from other bloggers. (Kevin Drum.)

Planning and producing a high-quality blog are important steps on the road to political blogging stardom. If you want to make it in the political blogosphere, however, you also need to promote what you're doing. If nobody knows that your blog exists, even the most compelling content in the world won't get you anywhere. As Jim Hoft puts it, "There are some excellent bloggers out there with terrific skills who people don't know about because they're not reaching out to other bloggers." Indeed, during my conversation with Eric Garris, he mentioned someone who, over the course of a year and a half, had invested $3 million in his blog but whose readership was dismal because he didn't have a clear idea on how to promote it.

The best way to promote your blog is to email links to your postings to other, more established bloggers in the hope that they'll link back to you in their own postings, thereby encouraging their readers to visit your blog. This is precisely what the world's most successful political bloggers did when they began blogging.

Established political bloggers are happy to repay the "debt" they incurred when they first started out, and have shared some tips on what you need to do to be taken seriously by them. First, it's important that you blog for a while, preferably at least a couple of months, before you start promoting your blog. A common mistake among new political bloggers is to promote their work prematurely. "New bloggers," according to Kevin Drum:

> tend to blast out emails and market themselves immediately, like in the first week of blogging. That almost never works. Established bloggers know that lots of people get into blogging and don't stick with it. So they don't get a lot of attention, because we all know that anybody who's blasting out emails trying to promote themselves after a week's worth of blogging is probably not going to be around in the next few weeks. So it's a waste of time. You need to do it for at least a few months.

Second, when you start forwarding links to your postings, make sure that you do so to the right people. "You have to identify people," says Matthew Yglesias, "who might be interested in what you're doing. You have to get in touch with them, possibly with individual posts that comment on what they're doing or they might be interested in." When doing so, it helps to personalize your communications rather than forward a generic email to everyone. "It impresses me," Jim Hoft emphasizes, "when I know that what somebody wrote was just for me. If the email is just for me, I'd certainly give it more attention than if I noticed somebody spammed 100 people with something they wrote."

Third, make sure to forward only your best postings and not everything you've written, and be sure that the links to those postings actually work. According to John Hawkins, too many new political bloggers send him what he bluntly refers to as "junk," because, as he speculates, "they simply don't know what else to do," and some people send him links to postings that don't work: "You click on the page, and there's nothing there."

Finally, be respectful when you approach other bloggers. In Jim Hoft's experience, many new political bloggers are less that respectful and, instead, expect that he'll "jump" for them.

While emailing links to your postings to more established political bloggers is the best way to promote your blog, you can also generate readers more directly by contributing to larger group blogs. As Heather Parton puts it, "If you become someone in the comment section that people value, they'll check out your own blog. It's sort of a relentless, yet subtle, attempt to get people to notice what you're doing." This is precisely what Parton did when she first started out. While contributing to Duncan Black's group blog, *Eschaton*, the other contributors were so impressed with her comments that they encouraged her to start her own blog.

Concluding Thoughts

> The political blogosphere is still very open to new participants, and you can go from zero to hero in a few months, which I think is great and really inspiring. (Nick Gillespie.)

Regardless of how you eventually decide to plan, produce, and promote your blog, be persistent and never give up. While some people will go from zero to hero in a few months, as Nick Gillespie puts it, others will find that it can take considerably longer to break through in the political blogosphere. A common mistake among new political bloggers, according to Matthew Yglesias, is to give up "too quickly on sites that are actually fine.

They don't understand that, by the nature of it, it takes a long time to build up an audience. In fact, if you've a site that any people are reading who don't know you personally, you're actually being fairly successful. These are people who're interested in it, and if you keep up the work that these people are interested in, you'll get a growing audience."

Good luck with your blog!

Notes

Introduction

1   Rebecca Blood, "Weblogs: A History and Perspective," in *We've Got Blog: How Weblogs are Changing our Culture*, ed. John Rodzvilla, Cambridge, MA: Perseus Publishing, 2002, pp. 7–16.

2   David Sifry, "State of the Blogosphere," *Sifry's Alerts*, August 7, 2006. Available online: www.sifry.com.

3   Kevin Wallsten, "Political Blogs: Transmission Belts, Soapboxes, Mobilizers, or Conversation Starters?" *Journal of Information Technology & Politics*, 4, 2007, pp. 19–40.

4   Matthew Hindman, *The Myth of Digital Democracy*, Princeton, NJ: Princeton University Press, 2009.

5   Richard Davis, *Typing Politics: The Role of Blogs in American Politics*, New York: Oxford University Press, 2009; David Perlmutter, *Blog Wars*, New York: Oxford University Press, 2008; Antoinette Pole, *Blogging the Political: Politics and Participation in a Networked Society*, New York: Routledge, 2010.

6   Wallsten, "Political Blogs."

7   Perlmutter, *Blog Wars*.

8   Kate Kaye, "Survey Shows the Blogosphere is Breaking Out," *ClickZ News*, April 26, 2006. Available online: www.clickz.com.

9   Perlmutter, *Blog Wars*.

10 Richard Davis, *Typing Politics*; William Eveland and Ivan Dylko, "Reading Political Blogs During the 2004 Election Campaign: Correlates and Political Consequences," in *Blogging, Citizenship, and the Future of Media*, ed. Mark Tremayne, New York: Routledge, 2007, pp. 105–126; Eric Lawrence, John Sides, and Henry Farrell, "Self-Segregation or Deliberation? Blog Readership, Participation, and Polarization in American Politics," *Perspectives on Politics*, 8, 2010, pp. 141–157.

11 Thomas Johnson and Barbara Kaye, "In Blogs We Trust? Deciphering Credibility of Components of the Internet Among Politically Interested Internet Users," *Computers in Human Behavior*, 25, 2009, pp. 175–182; Thomas Johnson, Barbara Kaye, Shannon Bichard, and Joann Wong, "Every Blog Has Its Day: Politically-Interested Internet Users' Perceptions of Blog Credibility," *Journal of Computer-Mediated Communication*, 13,

2008, pp. 100–122; Kaye Sweetser, Lance Porter, Deborah Chung, and Eunseong Kim, "Credibility and the Use of Blogs Among Professionals in the Communication Industry," *Journalism & Mass Communication Quarterly*, 85, 2008, pp. 169–185.

12 Kaye Trammell and Ana Keshelashvili, "Examining the New Influencers: A Self-Presentation Study of A-List Blogs," *Journalism & Mass Communication Quarterly*, 82, 2005, pp. 968–982.

13 Davis, *Typing Politics*.

14 Perlmutter, *Blog Wars*.

15 Hindman, *The Myth of Digital Democracy*.

16 Clay Shirky, "Power Laws, Weblogs, and Inequality," in *Extreme Democracy*, ed. Jon Lebkowsky and Mitch Ratcliff, 2005, pp. 46–52. Available online: www.lulu.com.

17 Davis, *Typing Politics*; Marcus Messner and Marcia DiStaso, "The Source Cycle: How Traditional Media and Weblogs Use Each Other as Sources," *Journalism Studies*, 9, 2008, pp. 447–463; Perlmutter, *Blog Wars*.

18 Henry Farrell and Daniel Drezner, "The Power and Politics of Blogs," *Public Choice*, 134, pp. 15-30.

20 Joel Bloom, "The Blogosphere: How a Once-Humble Medium Came to Drive Elite Media Discourse and Influence Public Policy," paper presented at the annual meeting of the American Political Science Association, Pennsylvania, 2003; Davis, *Typing Politics*; Kevin Wallsten, "The Blogosphere's Influence on Political Discourse: Is Anyone Listening?," paper presented at the annual meeting of the Midwest Political Science Association, Illinois, April, 2007.

21 Mark Glaser, "Trent Lott Gets Bloggered … Weblogs Credited for Lott Brouhaha." *Online Journalism Review*, December 17, 2002. Available online: www.ojr.org.

22 Peter Baker and Jeffrey Smith, "Miers Steps Down as White House Gears Up for Battle," *Washington Post*, January 5, 2007, p. A1; Elisabeth Bumiller and Carl Huse, "Bush's Court Choice Ends Bid; Conservatives Attacked Miers," *New York Times*, October 28, 2005, p. A1; Davis, *Typing Politics*.

22 Noam Cohen, "Blogger, Sans Pajamas, Rakes Muck and a Prize, *New York Times*, February 25, 2008, p. C1; Davis, *Typing Politics*; David Glenn, "The (Josh) Marshall Plan: Break News, Connect the Dots, Stay Small," *Columbia Journalism Review*, 46, 2007, pp. 22–27.

23 Perry Bacon and Shailagh Murray, "'Bitter' is a Hard Pill For Obama to Swallow," *Washington Post*, April 13, 2008, p. A1; Davis, *Typing Politics*; Katherine Seelye and Jeff Zeleny, "On the Defensive, Obama Calls His Words Ill-Chosen," *New York Times*, April 13, 2008, p. A1.

24 Jerome Armstrong, "A Victory For People-Powered Politics," *Christian Science Monitor*, November 9, 2006, p. A9; Jessica Clark and Tracy Van Slyke, *Beyond the Echo Chamber: Reshaping Politics Through Networked Progressive Media*, New York: Free Press; John Sides and Henry Farrell, "The Kos Bump: The Political Economy of Campaign Fundraising in the Internet Age," paper presented at the annual meeting of American Political

Science Association, Washington, D.C., August, 2010.

25   Davis, *Typing Politics;* Perlmutter, *Blog Wars*; Pole, *Blogging the Political.*

26   Davis, *Typing Politics*; Perlmutter, *Blog Wars*; Jose Vargas, "Net Roots' Event Becomes Democrats' Other National Convention," *Washington Post*, August 3, 2007, p. A4.

27   Davis, *Typing Politics*; John Garofoli, "Tech-Savvy Swarm of Bloggers Boosts Candidates' Online Presence," *San Francisco Chronicle*, November 3, 2007, p. A1; Perlmutter, *Blog Wars.*

28   Robert Bluey, "The Blog War on Capitol Hill," *Human Events Online*; January 2, 2007. Available online: www.humanevents.com; Eric Pfeiffer, "GOP Urged to Make Greater Use of Blogs," *Washington Times*, April 13, 2006, p. A9; Wallsten, "The Blogosphere's Influence on Political Discourse."

29   Davis, *Typing Politics*; Brian Faler, "A Capitol Hill Presence in the Blogosphere," *Washington Post*, October 11, 2005, p. A15; Eric Pfeiffer, "Bloggers Emerge as Force on Right; Briefings Pull Heavy-Hitters," *Washington Times*, August 15, 2007, p. A3.

30   Davis, Typing Politics; Perlmutter, Blog Wars; Gregg Sangillo, "Bloggers: A Who's Who," National Journal, January 21, pp. 37–39.

Index

CPSIA information can be obtained at www.ICGtesting.com
Printed in the USA
LVOW030712281011

252342LV00002B/4/P